"Before reading this book, I never completely understood how drugs kept people obsessively returning for more. Freddie's explanation of what drugs did for him made me grasp the "why." This is the first book I have read cover-to-cover — I could not put it down!

—TZUN TZUN THLUM GA (LOUISE SNOWDON) RPC, SOMATIC EXPERIENCING PRACTITIONER, SACRED TEACHINGS HOLISTIC COUNSELLING SERVICES

"In a world of fakes, this story's authentic and genuine ride was so exhilarating that I caught my breath and looked for a seat belt on my couch. It takes courage to be humble and open, like Freddie does in *Don't Judge Me*."

—GREG BUSHELL, ADDICTIONS COUNCILLOR AND AUTHOR

"Amazing! *Don't Judge Me* hits all the feels. Great words and easy to read. As a teacher, I think all teachers should read this! The stigma of drugs needs to change. Kids need to learn more about them, not just that drugs are bad."
—DENISE HENDRY, 4TH GRADE TEACHER

"Thank you for writing *Don't Judge Me* so honestly, as I truly think that's the only way we can get rid of the stigmatized perception of addiction."
—DAWNA HOPE, CHIEF, FIRST NATION OF NA-CHO NYÄK DUN, MAYO, YUKON

DON'T · JUDGE · ME

Husband · Father · Crack Addict

FREDDIE · WILSON

DON'T · JUDGE · ME

Husband · Father · Crack Addict

FREDDIE · WILSON

Above the Noise 2023

Library of Canada Cataloguing in Publication data is available.

ISBN 978-1-989528-23-5 (paperback edition)

ISBN 978-1-989528-24-2 (hardcover edition)

ISBN 978-1-989528-26-6 (e-book edition)

ISBN 978-1-989528-25-9 (PDF edition)

First Edition Printing 2023

Book cover artwork by Laura Lavender

Book design by Clint Hutzulak

Edited by Sofia Capel

Author photo by Tracy Wilson

Published in Canada by Above the Noise, New Glasgow, NS.

www.abovethenoisepublishing.com

For more information contact: publishing@abovethenoise.ca

Special discounts are available on quantity purchases by corporations, associations, and others. For details, contact the publisher at the address above.

For Dad

Contents

CHAPTER 1

Boyhood

1973, Terrace, Canada

I was lying on the living room couch, like most days, with my stomach facing the back of the couch and my arms stretched up over the top, when my mother entered the room.

"Whatcha doing, Freddie?" she asked and stroked my cheek. She followed my gaze and saw that I was watching the other children through the large bay window. They were all out on the street outside of our house, dozens of them, playing street hockey.

"Well," she said, "go on! Go out there and play!"

I didn't move from my spot. My six-year-old heart had already been trampled on too many times from trying to join in but always getting knocked back by them. "You're too young," they'd say, or "We're too many already!"

But Mom didn't give in. She was only five feet tall but as tough as boots.

"Go now!" she said, her voice stricter this time. "Do I have to take you up there?"

I reluctantly moved from the couch and went into the hallway, where I tied my shoelaces with heavy little fingers. Then I slowly trudged down the street to politely ask to join. I was prepared to get hurt again. Mom stood behind me with her arms crossed over her chest. She would not let her only son reach the age of seven without having grown a backbone. But sure enough, the kids, who were at least two years older than me, told me to get the hell out of there once more.

Terrace was a small, northern town in British Columbia, surrounded by snow-capped peaks, lakes, rivers, and deep forests. Despite only having a population of around 12,000, it was my whole world. The town had bloomed and became a city at one point, with a particularly young demographic, so the streets always echoed with the screams and laughter of kids playing sports. This was a time when children still played in the street. They'd drag a net onto the road, or if there was not a net at hand, they'd use two big rocks and a tennis ball, and whenever a car came along, they'd pause and remove the "goal" until the car had passed. Then the game would resume as if it had never been interrupted by the adult world. And every day, I looked at them and dreamt about joining the fun.

I had no brothers my age to play with, but I had three older sisters. There was Debbie, the oldest one. She was stocky and sometimes moody, and she would never let her siblings forget who their boss was. And then there were the twins, Ramona and Deanna, who were identical and every bit as gorgeous and popular as each other. They had rose blonde hair, high cheekbones, and the bluest green eyes. Even as their little brother, I would have to wait until they talked or moved because I would only be able to tell them apart by their mannerisms. Deanna was a bit of a goody-two-shoes and Ramona was a bit of a bad ass. The girls had a lot of fun being twins. They would switch boyfriends, as well as teachers. On exam day, Deanna would simply put on Ramona's clothes, sign in as her and do her test for her. Then she would stand up, excuse herself, and go to the bathroom. There she'd change into her own clothes, go back to the classroom, sign in as herself, and do the same test all over. The twins could fill a library with fun stories like that, they were always up to something crazy. They received lots of attention from boys. But Debbie was treated like the ugly duckling. Still, she was as tough as our mom and knew how to stand her ground.

I was the only grandson in a family full of granddaughters, and in a way, it made me feel special. My sisters and I would fight as siblings do, but I was lucky in the sense that if two of them were mean and nasty to me, a third one would always be nice and stick up for me. We had a pool table in the cellar, and we'd all play pool together when I had no one else to play with. Having older siblings meant that I was introduced to big kid stuff at an early age. They got me into cool bands like Led Zeppelin and Pink Floyd. I was the first one to bring *The Wall* to school. When I got a little bit older, they took me to see my first concert.

"Will you turn that noise down!?" our parents would shout from the kitchen whenever Debbie played her vinyl records in her bedroom. They were old school and preferred the melancholy, familiar melodies of country music to the new, angry cries of rock.

Despite the daily bickering and shouting, we were a happy family, and my parents were the best parents I could ever ask for. Mom and Dad were the two pillars that held up my whole world. My mom was a stay-at-home mom of Italian and Irish heritage. Every day when I came home after school, she'd have chores ready for me to do. My dad worked as a welder and was tall, stout, and square, like a reminder of the old cowboy days. He carried himself like a gentleman and was the type of man who would never swear in front of a woman, but always hold the door for her. He was a family man, a "Keeping up with the Joneses" kind of guy, always lending a helping hand whenever a neighbor needed something.

One Saturday morning, while lying on the couch in my usual position, I saw something new that caught my attention. I got up from my seat, walked up to the window, and pressed my face against it. The kid who lived across the street had been given a brand-new lawnmower motorcycle. He was just ripping around his yard, like a brave knight taming a wild dragon, and I couldn't stop watching him. The motorcycle was a monster, a machine, and a handsome steed all in one. I desperately wanted one of my own. "Dad!" I called. "*Daaad!*"

He came into the living room. "Dad, can I have one?" I said and pointed out the window. I knew my father adored me and always wanted me to be happy. But Dad shook his head in disbelief and said, "You're gonna have to wait until you're older to get one." So instead, I went over to my neighbor's house and asked to have a go. Next to hockey, motorbikes became my new obsession. Soon, most kids on the street had one.

In the summers, Dad would take six weeks off so that we could go camping around the different lakes of BC. My sisters would join us, until they got too old and "too cool" to go camping with us. As Mom got busy putting the tent up and preparing for lunch, Dad took me for a walk through the woods and taught me all about the different birds in the trees. When we went fishing, he taught me about the different fish in the water. And then he asked me the question that would every so often come up. "What would you like to be when you're all grown up, Freddie?" But of course, I didn't know. I just wanted my life to stay this way forever. Our house, our family, the forest, the lakes, the walks with Dad where he'd hold my hand and talk to me about the world. I didn't want anything else.

One late summer evening, after a vacation in the Kootenays, Dad was driving us back to Terrace in his four-door Plymouth. There was a lake on our left and a mountain on our right. I was in the backseat with my hands up on the ledge, looking out the back window, watching the waves on the lake disappear behind us. Suddenly, I spotted something like a long, black snake in the distance. "What on Earth is that?" I thought, as the snake approached us and got closer. And every time we turned a corner, I would look, and I could see the black snake coming closer. Soon, I began to feel a rumble, and I had to cover my ears from the noise. My mother's scream cut through all the noise.

"Pull over, Fred, PULL OVER!"

"It's ok, honey, I've got this," Dad said with a steady voice. But something in his voice was different, and I could sense that he was also scared. He kept looking in the back mirror as the massive snake was coming closer and closer. My sweet, strong, 280-pound dad was standing his ground. He was not going to pull over.

"It's a motorcycle gang!" Mum cried. She was now wrapping her arms around Dad's neck, on the verge of hysteria. "They're going to kill us!"

"Calm down, I said, I've got it!"

I knew I should be scared too, as it was unusual for my parents to act this way. Mom now turned around and started tugging at my shirt.

"Freddie, get down from the window, GET DOWN!" she cried.

But I couldn't stop staring. I was in awe. They were catching up to us now, and they were passing in a loud roar of thunder. There had to be about two thousand of them. Long hair, long beards, black shades, and tattoos that covered their bodies. They all had young women with big blonde hairdos on the back of their bikes, and as they went past, they saw the look on my mom's face. She was now screaming at me to stop looking at them. The girls loved it, smiled, waved, and gave us a thumbs up.

I was just a young, innocent boy from Terrace. I only knew about hockey players, loggers, and fishermen. I didn't know about bikers. The closest I had ever come to a motorcycle was those lawnmowers the neighbor kids all had. I had never seen anything like that in my life. It changed my world. It changed my perception of good and bad and what life could be about. My parents were so sure they were all bad people. But that was not what I saw. What I saw was freedom and people having a great time. I didn't realize it then, but that was me taking my first step away from my parents, understanding that we were not always going to feel the same way about stuff. When we came home, they sat me down and tried to explain to me that bikers were bad. They were bad people because they had tattoos and long beards. They could kill me if they wanted, my mother explained. But I didn't believe them. I was born again as a wannabe biker. My parents had taken their sweet, innocent boy on vacation and had come back with a little rebel. The bug was in me now, and it wasn't going away. I wanted a bike.

The next day, I went door to door and offered to wash my neighbors' cars, clean their basements, mow their lawns, and paint their fences. I did every job a little boy could do. I even got a job at a poultry farm about six blocks away. Looking back, I'm glad that my dad said no to buying me that lawnmower motorcycle because it showed me the value of working hard for the things I wanted.

A year went by, and by then I had finally saved up enough money to buy my own motorbike, a Yamaha. I was seven years old and felt really grown, tearing around on that thing. That whole summer, I ripped the fields up, playing around with my friends and our motorbikes. It had started with me, and then everyone followed. Lawrence was the next kid to get one, then my buddy Dave got a dirt bike, and then Harv got a dirt bike, and soon we were all going to a bigger field. I'd go around in a circle, make a jump, and rip around and around. Finally, a farm lady who lived near the field got sick of the noise and chased us around with a broom, but we just laughed. It was like a dream come true, and it was just the start. I knew that motorbikes were going to be in my life forever.

Once, we were doing a school play. We wrote the play ourselves, and it was about a motorcycle gang called The Falcons. We made patches and used them as props, and once the play was over, we kept them. "We're the Falcon club," we proudly proclaimed, although we grew out of that phase pretty quickly. I never really planned to belong to a motorcycle club, but I admired the freedom that seemed to come with it, and I wanted to be different. My dad was very much against that lifestyle.

"What would the neighbors think?!" he'd say whenever I pretended to be a bad ass biker. "They're gonna think you're into drugs!" But I shrugged him off. "People should like me for me, not for what I wear or look like," I said.

As my self-confidence grew, I tried approaching the kids playing hockey in the streets again. This time I was in luck because they were missing a player. By observing them from the couch for all those years, I had almost become an expert on how to play hockey without ever properly playing. I knew the moves. I knew where to go at the right time. These guys were always playing and turning the same way, so I turned the other way and scored a goal. And then I scored another one. It was constant, six or seven goals, to the point where everyone was gobsmacked. "Holy shit, kid!" one of them exclaimed. He had a mullet. They all had mullets. I wanted one too!

I played so well that they came banging on our door the next day, saying, "We need a goalie, Freddie, will you get in the net?"

They gave me a baseball glove as a mitt and used a tennis ball. The ball was wet, and when it hit me, it left big bruises, but I didn't care. It turned out I was a natural. Balls came flying toward me, and I caught them every time. They couldn't score on me. I was out there for hours, catching ball after ball. And I remember walking home, a mere 50 or 75 feet, but it was the walk of fame, with every kid in the neighborhood chanting my name.

"FREDDIE!"

"FREDDIE!"

"FREDDIE!"

When I finally got back into the house, my mom met me at the door. She had been watching me through the window the whole time. She saw me covered in brown stains and bruises and went,

"What the hell have you been up to?"

"I have been playing street hockey, Mom!" I said.

"How was that?" she asked with a smile.

"It was awesome!"

In 1974, a new arena opened in Terrace. It was the event of the decade, and I clearly remember queuing up by the doors, along with 800 other children.

After that, my parents always backed me with ice hockey. When the new arena opened, my mom volunteered to teach kids to skate. She would take me almost every day. After all, there wasn't much else to do. We lived in a very Northern community— one of the more isolated places in British Columbia. I decided I wanted to play hockey more often. My dad would get up at five o'clock, sometimes as early as four o'clock in the morning, and take me to practice. There were three or four practices a week, plus the games and then the traveling on the weekend, but they never complained.

And whenever the question popped up about what I wanted to be when I grew up, I always had the same answer: I wanted in the future what I had now. I wanted to ride motorcycles, and I wanted to play ice hockey. And I wanted a family, to be surrounded by the same type of beautiful people I was now, a nice wife, great kids. Just like my parents had been the pillars that held up my world, I wanted to become a dad and my children's safe place one day. Because my life was just perfect and I wanted the same wonderful rhythm to pulse through my veins for all eternity.

Then one day, one of my sisters came home, angry and confused because she had found out something about our parents. It turned out that they had kept a secret from us all our lives, a secret so dark it was meant to stay buried underground like a landmine. And the thing about landmines is, one day, someone will step on them, and they will blow up.

CHAPTER 2

Landmine

One late afternoon, I had just come home from hockey, and I was helping my mother set the table when Debbie barged in.

"Oh, good, you're back in time for dinner," Mom said while taking out the chicken from the oven, not looking directly at her.

"Freddie, will you go out and let your sisters know the dinner's nearly ready?" she said. Her back was turned to me, but I was staring at Debbie. The look on her face was indescribable. Her eyes were black like two bottomless wells. It was April, and Debbie had just turned 16. She was constantly nagging Dad to give her driving lessons. Unlike me, Debbie couldn't wait to get a car and get out of Terrace. Earlier that day, she had gone to register for a provisional driver's license.

Now she was standing by the kitchen door, holding a sheet of white paper in her hand.

"What is my name, Mom?" she asked sternly.

Slowly, our mother turned around and faced Debbie. For a moment, they just stared at each other without saying a word. Then Mom broke the silence in a small half-whisper.

"What do you mean?"

"What is my fucking name? My last name?" She threw the sheet of paper in Mom's direction, but it landed on the kitchen table, right in front of me. It was from the driver's license office. There were some numbers and letters that didn't make any sense to me, but at the top of the paper it said "Debbie Welch".

"Who is Debbie Welch?" I asked.

"THAT'S WHAT I'M FUCKING ASKING," she screamed.

Ever since I could remember, people had said that Debbie was her mother's daughter. I didn't know what it meant at first; of course, any girl is 'her mother's daughter'. But I later came to understand that they were talking about the similarities between them. They had the same short stature, same dark hair, and eyes. While the twins resembled Barbie dolls, their older sister was on the heavier side. She was not ugly, but I always thought she would be more beautiful if she didn't feel so awkward within herself. Unlike Mom, Debbie kept her hair cropped. When she furrowed her brow and stared deep into your eyes, she looked almost identical to our mother. But that was not where the similarities ended. Just like mom, Debbie was authoritative, almost on the verge of draconian. Perhaps it didn't matter that the twins were more popular, and I got more attention as the baby and only boy in the family because Debbie found power in being the oldest. Bossing us around seemed to be one of her few pleasures. She often seemed disgruntled and sometimes straight-up mean. If I ever beat her at pool, her eyes would narrow and go black, and she'd shout,

"MOM! FREDDIE'S CHEWING ON THE OLD FURNITURE AGAIN! COME GET YOUR SON!" or

"MOM, FREDDIE IS PLAYING WITH THE ELECTRICAL SOCKETS, TELL HIM TO STOP!"

As I was six and seven years younger than my sisters, my parents often used me to spy on them. Wherever they'd go, I'd follow, and then run back to Mom and Dad to report all the mischief they were doing. It couldn't have been very healthy for our relationship, because my sisters were getting tired of me always following them around. But even when they picked on me or treated me with the cruelty that only older siblings possess, I still loved the three of them dearly. And now, as Debbie was screaming at my mother in the kitchen, and my mother was trying to calm her down, promising that they would all sit down and talk about it when Dad came home, I understood that my picture-perfect family constellation was under threat. Then Deanna and Ramona walked through the door and demanded to know what was going on, and my mother just crumbled.

"Welch was your father's name. Your real father's."

The room went silent for a split second. Then I started crying. We had a real father who wasn't Dad? While the girls kept shouting at my mom, she quickly pulled me aside and said, "Dad is still your dad, sweetie. He's your dad but not your sisters' real dad."

By now I was utterly confused.

Later that evening, when my dad finally returned from work, we all sat down, and my parents finally opened up about the dark secret they had kept for all these years. Before meeting my dad, Mom had been married to another man. Debbie, Deanna, and Ramona were all that other man's children. When Debbie had gone to the driver's license office, they had asked her to provide her name and date of birth, but she had been told: "Your last name isn't Wilson, it's Welch." Not only had our parents lied to us that Dad was their dad, but he hadn't even adopted them. Their legal names were all Welch. Although I felt a slight relief at still being my dad's son, it was as if my parents changed shape across the dinner table, and became something smaller, more crooked, and foul.

For me, it wasn't so much about the blood relation. My sisters were still my sisters, regardless of who their father was. But to this day still, none of us can understand why my parents weren't honest with us from the start. Why lie? Why tell the school their names were Wilson, when we were likely to find out the truth later?

While I was still young, only eight, and my heart still open and my mind still naive, my sisters felt that their whole lives had been a lie. The screaming, shouting, and tears didn't end until much later that night, while I was in bed upstairs. After that day, everything changed.

Debbie, who had always been sullen and moody, was now carrying around a heavy load of anger wherever she went. The twins had gone from carefree and sweet to a pair of angry rebels. To say it was the spring of discontent would have been an understatement but Mom, Dad, and I did our best to carry on with our lives. My parents had four kids to feed, and the world needed to keep turning. Meanwhile, I had hockey, bikes, school, and friends to keep me occupied. I tried my best to feel happy and pretend that nothing had happened, but my parents' betrayal loomed over my head like a dark cloud. I was heartbroken.

When summer came, the three of us went on vacation in the Kootenays. The girls, now 15 and 16, had summer jobs and wanted to stay behind. Ramona had a boyfriend in Prince George, and it would have taken a herd of wild horses to pull her away from him. There wasn't much Mom or Dad could say for them to change their minds. Perhaps it was the guilt, but by now they were letting us get away with almost anything. My parents knew they could count on their friends and neighbors to check in on the girls while we were away. So, with that, we packed our bags, loaded them into the car, and took off for the summer.

In September, we arrived back to find the house in a state. Vinyls, empty beer bottles, and cans filled with cigarette butts were scattered all over our home. There was broken glass and weeks' worth of dirty plates on the kitchen counter, and our living room couch was pierced with cigarette burns. On it lay Ramona and her boyfriend, dazed and dead-looking. Mom went up to them and asked what the hell was going on. Ramona just shot her a look that said, "I'm not sorry," and closed her eyes to sleep. Later, when the girls were out of earshot, I heard my parents talking. Their voices were shaky and almost panicked.

"He brought *drugs* into our house!" my mother yelled. "She looked high as a kite!"

That was the first time I ever heard the word "drugs" uttered. I had no idea what it was, but I sensed that it was something very bad.

Once I was back in school the following week, the rumors started.

"I heard your sister is going out with a drug dealer from Prince George!" a boy in my year said to me.

"I heard he does smack!" said another.

"What's smack?" I asked.

"Heroin!"

The rumors reached Mom and Dad too, but by then, they were already suspicious of the girls' activity, so it was with a heavy heart that my dad left us for a week to go on his business trip. Deanna, Ramona, and Debbie all stayed away from the house as much as they could. When mom tried to talk to them, they'd snap at her and slam doors.

One night, the Saturday before my dad was due back, I was in bed, fast asleep. I was rudely awakened by the sound of doors slamming and high-pitched, angry voices. They were the voices of the twins and Debbie. It must have woken my mom up as well, or maybe she had been waiting up, but I heard her voice too.

"Fuck you, Mom!!" came the sound from downstairs. I sat up in bed, scared shitless. I had never heard my sisters so angry before. Then I heard thumping and my mom screaming for her dear life. It sounded like they were beating her up, and their voices were so foreign like they were possessed by demons. It was in pure rage and hatred they had come home to attack her. My whole room shook as they pushed my mom into the wall and then kept punching her and kicking her while roaring obscenities at her. "This can't be real," I thought. "This isn't happening."

I felt like such a piece of shit for not getting up and going down there to help my mom. Instead, I hid under the covers, wishing that it was all just a nightmare that I would soon wake up from.

Not even when the police arrived to arrest the girls did I dare to leave my room. I came down the next morning and found my mother full of bruises around her neck. She was bloodied and her face was red and swollen. I had never seen Mom look so defeated before. I understood that it was the drugs that had done this to my sisters. I knew that it was heroin that had turned them wild like a pack of rabid dogs. After that night, my sisters left home. They stayed in a caravan park somewhere, worked part-time jobs in retail, had boyfriends, and continued to do drugs.

The Very Bad Night left a long-lasting impression on the whole family. My parents often felt paranoid when I left the house. Every time I tried to go out to play with my friends, they'd ask me twenty questions. "Where are you going, who are you seeing, what will you do?" My friends would sometimes smoke doobies, which didn't bother me, but I wasn't interested in trying.

My parents knew that the kids in our town started with drugs and alcohol early, so one day, while I was still only nine, my dad sat me down and made a deal with me.

"You can never, ever do drugs in this house. If you have taken drugs, you are not welcome in this house. You can drink, but you can't do drugs. If you want to do drugs, you must wait until you're 18. That is all I ask of you, Freddie."

I thought for a while, then I said, "So I can drink because it's socially acceptable and legal, but I can't do drugs because it's not socially acceptable and not legal. Right?"

"Right."

"So, I can smoke too? Cigarettes are legal."

"No Freddie, you're nine, for God's sake! You're not allowed to smoke cigs."

"Then there's no deal!" I shot back at him.

I tortured my dad for two whole days with this, until he sat down with me again and said, "Okay, I gotta conclude our meeting. The deal is, you can drink. I'll even buy you the booze. You can smoke cigarettes, but I don't wanna see it. I don't wanna see you smoking, but I know you're gonna be doing it. It's fine. But no drugs under my roof."

I made the deal and shook his hand.

The fallout of the great revelation and the Very Bad Night had changed me. I grew up very fast after that. I walked around, on edge, almost like I was preparing myself for whatever to just come outta the blue and hit me sideways. I had my guard up now. The nasty rumors about my sisters were still going around.

"I heard Debbie is selling her butt underneath the overpass," one older boy said as I walked past him. I was getting used to comments like that, but they hurt all the same. I told him to shut his big old face.

I remember feeling confused a lot of the time. I saw adults chugging wine and beer and getting awfully loud and ill-looking from it. Even kids my age were drinking beer and smoking pot, and no one ever said anything about it. You could buy beer and wine in the shop just like you could buy milk and toilet paper, but my sisters were doing something called "drugs" and therefore they had to leave home and live in a trailer. There were also these places called "drug stores" where folks would get their drugs that were legal, to make them feel better. It seemed there were drugs that made you sick and drugs that made you healthy, and there was wine that made you sick but the housewives on the street drank it daily, nonetheless. You can imagine the added confusion when they said on the radio that Elvis had died of a heart attack that was "likely brought on by his addiction to pharmaceutical drugs." So many things just didn't make sense anymore!

I turned ten and spent most of my time with my friends Harvey and David. They'd sit and smoke pot while I drank beer and smoked cigarettes. Harv, who was a loud and rowdy know-it-all, always knew where to get hold of some. Dave, whose parents had just divorced, had gone quiet, weird, and occasionally mentally unstable. We could be playing pool, and suddenly, he'd have a fit and start throwing pool balls all around him. A lot of the kids were like that in Terrace. Despite all its natural beauty, it was a hard place to grow up, hyper-masculine. Most of our dads were big loggers, all making decent money and most of them drank. Drugs and booze were everywhere. We all still got along, though, despite the climate.

The older I got, the more attracted I was to the more edgy lifestyle I had seen in music magazines and on the road. I grew my hair longer and longer, and my parents hated it. My mom nagged me to cut it, and I finally gave in. Reluctantly, I sat down in the chair with a great huff. Mom started cutting, but I wouldn't let her cut my hair above the ears. I had big ears and didn't want them to stand out. "Mom, stop!" I whinged and shook my head a bit to get her off me. Then I felt a sharp sensation in my ear. Mom had cut off my earlobe! I just shrieked. "Mom, you cut me!" I shouted at her.

"It's your fault!" she shouted at me back. "I thought the scissors were stiff and it's your fault that I did it because you're so insistent that I can't go shorter than the bottom of your ear."

The bottom of my earlobe was hanging and dangling, so she got a Band-Aid and said, "There, now shut up you little bugger!"

That was it for me. I never let her cut my hair after that. Besides, I wanted a mullet like all my friends had. I kept cutting bangs and leaving the rest of my hair to grow. It made me feel like a real badass. I decided that no one was gonna get away with messing with me from here on.

In school, there was a new kid from outta town. He had gone through the foster system and pretty much got kicked out of every house in Prince Rupert. So he had been shipped to Terrace. I would see him making his way around the school, picking on different kids. One day it ended up being my turn. The little fucker squared up to me and put his finger in my chest. And just when I thought that Dave and Harv would have my back, they started joining this dickhead in bullying me. I just lost it and went completely ballistic. I grabbed him and started straight-arming him. And the whole time, I was yelling at my friends, "I'm gonna fucking kick your ass too. You fucking bastards."

It won me the respect of all the other kids. "Did you see Freddie?" I heard them whisper. "He just fucking lost it. Like fucking lost it. Don't fuck with him."

That day, I walked home with my head up and my chest out. I went in and told my mom that this was my new lifestyle, being a badass. The next day we were going on a field trip with school, and somebody had a track player. The music started blaring, and it shook me to the core. I could feel horns grow out of my forehead and a devil's tail coming out of my ass. "Holy fuck!" I said. "What is this music?"

It was AC/DC. Listening to them was like being born again, but in the church of Satan. My friends and I all started wearing t-shirts and patches with the band's logo sewn onto the backs of our denim jackets. My parents absolutely hated it and called it "devil's music", but I didn't care. No other bands did music justice. Listening to it felt like coming home.

CHAPTER 3

Shaping up

My friends and I mostly amused ourselves by getting drunk in the gravel pits and occasionally going bear-spotting at the dump. When we got a little bit older, we would drive the five hours to Prince George to scout the record shops for new music. We rarely left satisfied, as the sound of the 80s didn't reach our part of the world until the 90s, apart from a few golden nuggets. But Prince George had three shopping malls and was a real metropolis in our eyes.

Every now and then, Dad would take me to see my sisters. After the Very Bad Night, they had moved into a trailer on the outskirts of town. Dad had really meant it when he said he would never accept any drug-taking under his roof. Seeing the state of them, obviously still hooked on drugs, made my stomach turn. I didn't understand how they could live like that, in a dirty trailer, in what was more or less a swamp. But when she was 17, Ramona called Mom at home with some unexpected news. She was getting married! She had met a decent guy, drug-free and without any ill intentions. They had fallen in love, and soon they would also start their own family.

She managed to get back on track through the path of motherhood. Deanna came back home for a little while to finish school then met a young police officer and got married as well. Debbie never came back, but she held her own, working hard and managing just fine without us.

Harv was still a crazy fucker. One day, I was waiting for the bus with some pals when I heard a roaring motor. It was Harv, speeding down the road in his dad's truck. We were 14 at the time. He went all over the road, hit the brakes, broke a fence, and slid into a ditch. Then he came out of the ditch and stopped right in front of me. "Hop in!" he shouted with a face like a cheeky beaming sun. So a few of us got in, and we just ripped the street up. Harvey never got caught for some reason, which made it even more fun to hang out with him.

Since my dad let me drink, I sometimes came home drunk. I'd sneak in as discreetly as possible, with the grace and decorum of a moose in heat. One late night, coming back, the house was completely dark. I walked across the hall and stumbled over my own shoes, making lots of ruckus. When I got to the stairs, there was a dark shadow standing at the very top. I made my way up the stairs and saw the stern face of my mother, with her arms crossed over her chest.

"Come here, Freddie," she said, calmly. As I tried to push past her, she kicked me down the stairs. I tried to crawl up the stairs, but this time, she kicked me in the head. She was wearing boots, and I later realized that she must have put them on only to kick me. I tried one final time to just push past her, but she kicked me once more, and I gave up.

"You're as drunk as a skunk!" she hissed. "You're sleeping on the couch tonight!"

"You're... probably right," I slurred.

That was just my mom, as tough as the boots she used to kick the shit out of me.

Anytime AC/DC were playing, we'd drive down to Vancouver to see them. We had a friend who had moved there, so we would crash at his place after the concert was over. In Vancouver, there was a tattoo parlor called The Dutchman, known around town and probably, the world. We'd stand outside with big eyes and peek at the people coming out with fresh tribal tattoos on their biceps, fire-breathing dragons, and band logos inked on their backs and legs. All our idols had tattoos, and I just knew I had to get one too. But I needed an adult signature, and there was no way my parents would ever let me.

"Grandad will do it!" Harvey said with a cheeky grin. Harvey's grandad was an Indigenous man and someone I got along great with. I had spent a weekend with his family a year prior, where I had got his respect by showing a lot of interest in Indigenous culture. Once we were back home again, we sat down with Harvey's grandad and explained that we were all getting inked to honor First Nations culture, and he gladly gave his signature. The following weekend we all tumbled out of the Dutchman, with our spirit animals forever engraved in our skin. Mom found out, but we agreed not to tell Dad.

It was around that time that I felt that I was done with just hanging around with my buddies. I had matured a lot and felt like I should be doing something more productive with my life. Dad didn't like that I had grown my hair long and had tattoos. He hated the music I listened to and thought I had become a devil worshipper. "Just wait until you're asleep, and I'll come into your room and chop that hair off," he'd jokingly threaten. We were two very different people, him and me, but the love was still there. Despite not liking my lifestyle, he got me my first real motorbike for my birthday that year and let me ride it to our summer vacation spot.

When winter came, Dad, who was now my coach, took me to try out for the Kitimat Blackhawks junior B team. We probably went to about five or six try-outs, and I was doing quite well, apart from the fact that I would get the shit kicked out of me.

These guys were big, and they were fast, and I couldn't keep up. They'd go between the ice rink and the gym daily, whereas I just didn't have that dedication. It was a tough league and a tough try-out with a lot of scraping, especially for me. I was a thinker, and small but quick. They would take me out and thump me. One day I got into a bad fight. As we were in juniors, we didn't have to wear proper helmets that protected our faces, and this guy pushed his baby finger into my eye socket. He pushed and pushed, blood splattering everywhere. Nobody had a clue about what he was doing—it just looked like we were fighting. I freaked out, screamed, "You motherfucker, I'll rip your face open!!" and did just that. I stuck my two fingers up each one of his nostrils. And I tore up towards his eyeballs, and I ripped the skin from his nose all the way up. It bled everywhere, unbelievable amounts of blood all over his jersey and all over the ice.

In the car, going back home with dad, we agreed that was the end of my hockey career. I knew he would have supported me if I had chosen to continue, but deep inside, I knew that it was a waste of time. A few years earlier, my dad had asked me, like he used to do every so often, "Tell me, Freddie, what do you want to do with your life?"

"I want to play in the NHL!" I responded. But Dad just shook his head and smiled.

"That's dream talk, Freddie!" he had said. "You'll have a better chance of winning the lottery!"

Hockey just wasn't fun anymore. The feeling it had given me ten years prior, as I walked home while everyone was shouting my name, had faded. Maybe it was always about earning people's respect for me. I craved that respect and suspected that I always would. But it wouldn't come from playing ice hockey. Many of my friends continued to play. Their parents supported them, and eventually, a few of them ended up in the NHL. It's funny what you can achieve when you don't give up on your dreams.

I ended up getting work at a Chevron gas station across the river. It was known around town that the owner, Ralph, was just out of jail for murder. Luckily, he worked at one of his other stations, so instead, I got to work with Al. Al, or Big Al as I called him, was a large, bald man with a big old beard, and he smiled the biggest smile I had ever seen when he shook my hand. Big Al was quite a drinker. He always had a big bottle of Wisers in the office, which was on the other side of the wall from where I was standing. Every night while Al was doing the books, he was thumping his fist on the desk and screaming, fuck, fuck, fuck. The customers would hear every word, so one evening, I popped my head in and hissed,

"Al! I'm trying to serve customers out here!"

"Sorry!" he slurred. "It's just that I'm trying to do these books and keep them in place. Money's out, and it's just fucking frustrating!"

"Give me a moment, and I'll have a look at it," I said. I had never handled books before, but I thought that if a pisshead like Al could be trusted with it, so could I.

I finally sat down and said, "You're fucking half-cracked all the time. That's why you're fucking it up. Teach me to do it instead. Just tell me when a car comes in, I'll run out of the office, serve the car, and then come back to work on the books."

So Big Al taught me all he knew, how to run the till tapes, how to do the log, the hours, and liters. We ended up shutting down one of the bays in the garage area and creating a convenience store instead. We had some coolers in there and bought hot dogs and sandwiches. As simple and uneventful as it sounds, it was a great experience for me, jobwise. I always assumed being around capable adults was good for teenagers, but it turned out that being around incapable drunkards was even better! It forced me to take control and responsibility and acquire a set of skills.

I did the books for Al for about six months, and after that, he got a job as a bear blaster, a much more suitable job for a guy like Big Al.

"Who will be my boss now?" I thought. That's when it hit me: it was Ralph, the murderer, who was gonna take over.

The day he was coming in, I was shaking in my boots. I had pictured a mafioso-type fellow but was surprised when Ralph walked through the door. He came in with a big smile on his face and said, "Al says you're a fucking phenomenal guy!"

"Um... Hi, thanks!" was all I could say.

"I know you're only 16, but I want to give you the opportunity. You're gonna manage the gas station. I'm gonna pay you good money."

I was lost for words.

So at 16, I became the manager, and I worked with that for a year and a half. After that, Ralph sold the gas station to the bread man who used to do the bread deliveries every week. His name was Gary Alger, and his wife was Mary. When they came to see me, they said, "Hi, we are the new owners. And for a dollar, we would like you to be one of the owners with us."

I couldn't believe my ears, but they said they wanted to call the company MFG, "Mary, Gary, and Fred". They wanted to split profits with me, and I still got an hourly wage.

Things were almost going too well for me. I was about to graduate high school and was already co-owner of the station. But my dad wasn't impressed. As always, he wanted to know: "Freddie, what do you want to do with your life? Surely you don't want to work in a gas station for the rest of your days?"

It was a rude awakening, but he was right. The money was good, and I also knew that there was more to life than this. I wanted to travel and experience the world. Up until then, the isolated northern community of Terrace had been my whole world. I knew every bump in the road, driving from my parents' house to Remo. I knew every creek, field, stone, tree, shop, man, woman, and child.

Now I wanted to hop on my motorbike and drive off toward the horizon, see new places and meet new people. I wanted to go to theaters and bars and walk barefoot on hot sand. I wanted to experience the world I had seen on TV, especially the music videos. I had seen Prince ride around on his purple motorcycle, and I wanted to feel how I felt listening to "When Doves Cry." More than anything, I wanted to go out in the world and earn the respect of people, like I had earned respect in my hometown. That feeling of people chanting my name and whispering about me when I went past, was addictive. Terrace wasn't enough for me anymore.

I came home after grad weekend and was welcomed by my father at the door. "Come in, son, I have a surprise for you!" he said.

We sat down, and he handed me an envelope. I noticed that his hand was shaking a little bit. I opened it: it was a one-way bus ticket to St John's, Newfoundland.

"You've told me you wanted to see the world," Dad said solemnly, "and if you look closely in the envelope, there's a $50 bill in there, as well as the address of a friend of mine."

He continued, "I've already contacted this guy. He's got a fish canning plant in St. John's, Newfoundland, and he'll give you a job and room and board, just contact him when you get there." He made a dramatic pause. "But... if you wanna get off the bus sooner, cos it's gonna take you about five and a half days to get there, use these $50 and see the world."

"Wow, thanks, Dad!" I said, a bit taken aback.

"One more thing..." Dad said, "the bus leaves at 1!"

I jolted out of my seat, ran upstairs, and packed my most important belongings into a backpack. Then I kissed my parents goodbye and went off on my adventure. But I never made it to St. John's.

CHAPTER 4

Tracy

My journey through Canada was amazing. It was full of partying, drinking, and meeting lots of interesting people. As soon as I stepped off the coach in Ontario, a guy walked up to me and said, "Hey, you got any weed?"

"What? No, I don't have weed."

"Where are you from?"

"Terrace, BC."

"There you go, you've got long hair, and you're from Terrace, you gotta smoke weed!"

But I had kept my promise to my dad, and I was still a little bit afraid of drugs. On that journey, however, I tried pot for the first time. It was good, but I didn't feel addicted to it. I preferred getting drunk. The reason I stayed in Ontario for a while was that my sister Debbie lived there. She still had problems with drugs. She had gone from using heroin to abusing pharmaceutical drugs instead. She would go to the doctor and demand pills, and she would get them. It wasn't great seeing her like that, and it put me off drugs even more.

I returned home to BC soon after that and by then I knew my drinking had reached new heights and I should cut back. I really wanted to focus on finding myself. I was 19 and wanted to figure things out. So I did six weeks of AA. It may surprise you that after I finished rehab, I went on to take a bartending course! But I did. And despite never sampling any of the cocktails I made, I ended up scoring a whole 99%. I figured I didn't have to sit at home every night like a boring old fart just because I wasn't drinking anymore.

On the back of that, I applied for a job at a newly opened pub in Nanaimo, the "sin city". The ad stated that the applicant needed to have at least two years of experience. I showed up on the day of interviewing, where I met Jerry Franco, an Italian dude from Vancouver. He looked me up and down and asked, "How old are you?"

"I'm 19."

"So how can you have two years' experience, kid?"

"Well, I don't!"

"So what the hell are you doing here?"

"To tell you that's not a very smart way of hiring people in this business."

Jerry was smirking now, amused.

"What do you mean?"

"You want them to have experience because you want them to know what they're doing. But you also don't want them to know how to skim from you, which most experienced bartenders do."

Jerry opened his mouth. I quickly fished up my certificate.

"Look," I said. "I got 99% in the bartending course that says I'm a certified bartender. All I know how to do is everything by the book. I don't know how to cheat. I don't know how to skim. So, if you wanna hire people with those habits, go ahead. If you wanna hire somebody who just knows how to bartend, I know how to bartend. And I'd like you to consider me."

The next day he called me in and gave me the job as head bartender.

The only guy above me was Rick. He was the bar manager, a real ladies' man, and big on the booze. Just like with my first job, the manager didn't last too long. The Francos came over from Vancouver and sat me down and offered me the job of manager.

"We'll teach you how to do the books," they said.

"Never mind," I said. "I already know how to do them."

So I ran the bar and managed the pub, and it was all going great. I was working one early afternoon when the door opened, and a young woman came in alone. As soon as she stepped into the bar, the whole place fell silent. The row of men who were heaving beers stopped in their tracks and turned around to look at her. She had a big blonde perm, a little black skirt on, and high heels. All I could think was, "Holy shit." She looked like one of those biker chicks I had seen when I was a kid.

She walked straight up to the bar and said, "Hi there! I see you're looking for a waitress."

"Um..." I said.

"I've got experience."

"Uuhh..."

She raised one eyebrow. She had the bluest eyes I had ever seen, tastefully decorated with blue eyeshadow.

"May I speak to the manager?"

"I... I am he. Yes. I am the manager," I managed to stutter.

She looked at me like I was the biggest fool on the planet.

"Okay..." she said, "Well, here's my resume. Please consider my application." She strutted out again. Once she was out of earshot, the row of men burst out laughing.

"Holy shit, Wilson, get your tongue back in your mouth!"

But I was spellbound. Meeting Tracy was like getting smashed in the face with a fucking baseball bat. I was in love.

Three days later, she came back in. She approached me at the bar and slammed her hands down on the counter. "Hello again!" she said. "Why haven't you called? You need a waitress; I need a job. What's the problem?"

Her cocky, confident attitude was too much.

"Come with me," I said and took her into my office. I sat her down.

"Look, I can't hire you."

"Well, why the hell not?"

"I can't even *speak* when you're around me! You're too beautiful! How about we go on a date instead?" I asked, awkwardly.

"How about you give me a job?!" she shot back, smiling. "And we'll see about that date."

And that was it. From the first shift, we were inseparable. She asked for a ride home and I complied. We spent the whole night talking. We spent every night together after that, but we didn't even have sex, we just talked. It was important to her that we became friends first, before we could be lovers.

One month after Tracy walked into the pub, I took her out on a date at the Queens. It was a country night, which I would normally hate, but sitting there with her, chatting away, drinking Coca-Cola, it still felt like the best night of my life. At the end of the evening, I just grabbed her face gently and kissed her. "I love you," I said, and she said it back. Three months after first meeting, we were engaged. Another three months in, we were married. We knew we wanted to have a family straight away. We had Jessie in '91 and Jaz in '92; the most beautiful gifts we could ever have dreamed of.

I ended up leaving the job where we had first met, to pursue a college course in welding. As my father had been a welder, he had taught me the trade from a young age, and I thought I wanted to follow in his footsteps. But once I graduated, I was faced with the harsh reality: the jobs paid a meek ten bucks an hour for welding handicap reels into washrooms. I couldn't find any other jobs until I stumbled on an ad in the paper: *Bar staff wanted, The Globe Hotel, Nanaimo.*

I was familiar with the Globe. It was the level B strip club where the Hells Angels hung out. I showed the ad to Tracy, and she shrugged, "Bartending is bartending. Go for it!"

I went for the job, remembering my parents' words about the Hells Angels. "They are dangerous people, they will kill you, given the chance!" I was feeling intimidated, walking in for the interview, not sure what to expect. But no biker jumped out from behind the counter to slit my throat, so I told myself I was off to a good start.

The Globe was a very old venue and looked like something from the old cowboy days. It had two big black saloon doors on the front, and when you entered, you were standing right in front of the stage. I kept my head down every day, and served construction workers, bikers, and undercover cops. I also DJ'd, announcing the girls on and off stage, did the lights, and music. The money was half-decent; on a slow day, I'd make maybe sixty dollars, and on a busier day, I'd make maybe a hundred bucks on tips. I had slowly started drinking again, but more carefully this time. It was more of a social thing. By now, I had also experimented with mushrooms. I was beginning to understand that trying drugs wasn't gonna be the end of the world. I just did it carefully, not to get hooked on anything, like my sisters had.

Every day, a man called Eric would sit at the end of the bar with his back to the restrooms. He was always watching everyone, like a hawk. I especially felt like he was watching *me*. Guests would walk past him on their way to the bathrooms and tap him, and he'd discreetly hand them stuff. But I minded my own business, kept my head down, and swept the floors. Maybe that's why, one night after closing, Eric asked me and a few others to stay for drinks.

"Do you mind staying for a bit, and we'll just run a notepad of how many drinks and then just ring them in tomorrow?" he said, "I'll pay you in cash."

So I started staying late for a few nights in a row. I could tell that there was something going on; everyone seemed stressed out. But I didn't ask, I kept my head down as usual. Finally, Eric confided in me.

"We've got an audit," he said through gritted teeth. The books didn't match the till tapes.

They had taken these till tapes and said they were up in the attic and that there was a water leak. They had soaked them all down with a hose and given them to the auditors. The books were, of course, water damaged, but it didn't fly. They were now in big trouble.

I just looked at Eric. I realized I knew something he was completely oblivious to.

"Well... Why don't you just redo the till tape?"

"What...? What the fuck are you talking about?"

Because of my experience at the Chevron and the Landlubber, I knew all the ins and outs of tills and books. All tills came with two keys, one key would work for X and Y. X gave you a subtotal for the day, Y would cash out the till at the end of the day.

The other key was a master key which would work for X and Y but also went to Z. Z mode would allow you to program the till, including date and time — or to clear your whole day.

I offered to fix the problem for them, as it was something I could get through in a few nights.

Within three or four days, they had all their till tapes matching for the whole year, all the way through to their ledger. And they presented the books to the auditors, and it was flawless.

I had saved the day, and, probably, the whole hotel. With it came the respect I had dreamt of for so long. I was the man now. They patted me on the back, insisted on buying me drinks, and called me the fucking king. It felt like being back on the street outside my house, when I was walking home, and everyone was chanting my name. My tips rose from about sixty to three hundred bucks a day.

One evening a customer got drunk and rowdy. When I told him I wasn't gonna serve him any more beer, he challenged me to a fight.

"Sure, let's go outside, big boy!" I yelled.

We stepped out of the bar out onto the sidewalk. This guy turned around and went to lift his fist to me. Somebody's fist went over the top of my shoulder and fucking cracked this guy's face. He did one of those cartoon 360s and flew down on his back. I turned around to see who threw their fist over my shoulder, but there was nobody there. Everyone at the Globe Hotel knew you don't mess with Freddie. And they were gonna have my back.

It was July, and the annual Angel Acres parties were taking place in Nanaimo. It is an event where hundreds of Hells Angels members from all over the world come together.

I was working my normal shift when some of the boys came in. They went up onto the right-hand side of the bar and sat down. Between them and the stage were the undercover cops, drinking Labatts Blue. On the left of me sat three European tourists drinking Heineken. It was normal for me to observe the drinkers in the pub. You never knew what would go down in a place like this.

After an hour or so, a man dressed like a chauffeur came in and sat with the guys from Hells Angels.

"Limo ready?" one of them asked him.

"Yes, the limo is ready for you when you've finished your drinks," the driver responded politely.

After a while, they all stood up and left. Then I heard a commotion outside the hotel. I ran out to check what was going on. The limo had been stolen! I went back in, and the undercover cops were already all over it, with their little flip phones out.

I looked around the pub. The Europeans had left. They were the only ones I could tell had left the hotel in the last hour. I immediately got on the phone and called up the Balmoral, the rival strip club on the other side of town.

"Hey if you see three European guys coming in and ordering Heineken, could you check outside if there's a limo with them? It's a stolen car."

The guy on the phone said, "Yep, they just came in! Let me check the parking!"

Sure enough, the cheeky buggers had stolen the limo and driven off to the next strip joint!

Within five minutes, he called back.

"Freddie, I got the fucking keys. They have the car out there. I've got the guys sitting in the office with me."

I hung up the phone and went to get Eric. He growled at me to fuck off and not bother him as he was busy trying to find the limo before we were all in some deep shit. The president's limo had been stolen on our turf.

"But I've got the limo back, and I caught the guys who did it!" I shouted.

He just stared at me. I didn't see Eric for about three days after that. When I saw him again, he wanted to invite me to the clubhouse to say thanks. It was the hotspot for all the Hells Angels, not exactly a club anyone could just walk into.

Eric had his arm around me and shouted at anyone within a two-mile radius that I was the man, I was the top guy at the Globe. He bought me drinks all night. He introduced me to the different members of Hells Angels and told them that I was the guy who got the limo back. It was amazing to feel so celebrated and respected by all these big guys who I had been taught to fear. They all seemed like genuinely great people, not the blood-thirsty thugs my parents had warned me about. It was empowering to understand something that my parents never did understand. It made me feel like a more knowledgeable person and that I would never have to fear people again. Hell, it made me feel like I could overcome any of my fears in life. I had craved acceptance since I was a child, and I had finally won it. It felt good. From that night on, I was Eric's best friend. With him, I got even more respected and admired as he was someone everyone feared. Yes, by now, I was on a high, high cloud.

"You've got a room at the hotel anytime you like, ok?" he said to me with a breath full of booze.

"That's great!" I said, "Thanks, buddy!"

"Do me a favor, pal," he discreetly handed me a flap, "hold on to this for me. No matter how drunk I get, don't let me have it. I trust you."

I took the bag and put it in my pocket.

"Absolutely!" I told him, and I held onto it all night, because, as everyone at the Globe knew: you don't say no to Eric.

CHAPTER 5

Whirlpool

Eric had a problem with crack. It wasn't exactly a secret, but when it came to stashing his gear, I was the only one he trusted. I wasn't into drugs — everyone knew that. Yes, I had experimented on a couple of occasions, but I had never been hooked on anything.

In the morning, I woke up in the hotel room and didn't know where I was at first. Then came a knock on the door and Eric's voice shouting, "Hey Freddie, open up." Then I remembered the previous evening when I had met the Hells Angels and agreed to hold onto Eric's stash for him. Tracy had said that if I was gonna stay out late, I might as well crash at the hotel, so I didn't wake the kids coming back home. She was cool with it and trusted me to behave.

I opened the door to Eric. He looked sick, with his face pale and his forehead sweaty.

"Do you have it?" he asked, his hands shaking.

"Yeah, don't worry, I've got it."

"Where is it?"

"It's where I keep all my important stuff," I grinned. "In my boot."

"IN YOUR BOOT?!" Eric punched the wall. I stopped grinning.

"You fucking idiot, you can't put it in your fucking boot!" he roared.

"Why not? I just put it in my sock, and no one will think to steal it from me."

"Because the sweat from your fucking feet will fuck up the stuff!"

I got my boot out and opened the flap. It looked like snot, gooey and damp from the moisture in my socks.

Eric scared me. He was breathing heavily now, as if he was about to open his awful mouth and swallow me whole. I had to think on my feet.

"Fuck. Okay. We can fix this. Fuck. We can fix this," I said, "We can get a cookie sheet, fuck, we'll spread it out really thin on the cookie sheet, put it in the oven at a low heat, and cook the moisture out of it."

"You fucking idiot," he growled, "you can only fix this one way. You go get me a bottle of fucking ammonia. They sell it at the store."

He didn't have to tell me twice. I ran to the shop and got what we needed. When I came back, Eric said: "Come here, I'll fucking teach you."

He put the goo on a spoon and added sudsy ammonia, and the stuff started bubbling up. He cooked it over the stove, shaking the spoon, and all this shit was coming up. And then he ran it underneath the tap. There was this liquid ball on the bottom of the spoon, and he took a pin and got it underneath cold water. Then he kept stirring it and stirring it until the ball dried up on the end of the pin. And it was a hard white fucking ball of crack.

He looked up at me and said, "Fuck it, you caused this fucking situation, you're doing it with me."

I took a deep breath. A few months prior, Tracy and I had been invited to dinner by the hotel owner. There we had been offered to try "speed". We had thought it meant "bennies", little speeders my sister used to take. When we realized that it meant crystal meth, Tracy stepped back and was cool with me doing it, and the next day I had felt fine. I didn't get addicted and hadn't had the urge to do it again. So now, standing in front of Eric, I thought, *I'm just gonna do this with him, pay my dues, get home, have a good night of sleep, and life is gonna go on.*

Eric lit a cigarette, gave it to me, and said, "Don't smoke it. Put it in the ashtray and wait for the whole ash to become a nice, pure, clean ash. Get the pipe, put a little screen in the bottom, fill it with that nice clean ash, and put some of that rock into it." I did what he told me.

Then he said: "You have to use a match; it has more heat than a lighter. I'm gonna start warming this up. You exhale. And then when I tell you to inhale, I'm gonna hit this with a match, and you're gonna inhale." He said this all with a kind of reverence as if we were at some twisted church. I nodded.

"Okay, hit it."

And I started sucking. Eric put that match on the rock, and it slowly burned perfectly down in the middle of the ash. I inhaled, inhaled, inhaled until there was nothing but ash left. And when I exhaled, the taste was something I would never forget. It was like a burning coconut, fucking phenomenal. As soon as I exhaled, my back hit the wall, and my ass hit the floor. I felt like I was strapped to the end of a rocket ship, piercing the atmosphere and sending me into the universe.

My whole brain lit up like a Chilean Christmas tree. I was using so much of my mind, and I could completely understand things that I had never understood before in my life.

"Woah..." was all I could say. And then, "Eric... Woah... it's fucking incredible."

Even as I was slowly coming down, and coming closer to earth, I felt superhuman. My sight, my thoughts, my ears... all my senses peaked. Time was moving faster, and I was moving with it like I had jets on my heels. The night was quick. My movements were quick. My thoughts were quick. Meanwhile, my understanding of people and how they're living and what they're going through, it all made sense. I had reached nirvana. A feeling so great overcame me to the point where I had to tell Tracy about it. I had to tell my friends about it. I had to get them to experience this with me. *You have no idea what the fuck you're about to experience,* I thought, trembling from the dopamine rush.

The hit lasted for about ten minutes. *I've done what I had to do,* I thought. *Now I should go home and get a good night's sleep.* But I didn't make it home. As I was collecting my things to leave the hotel, I started to come down heavier. Now I felt like everything had come down to a slow, almost crawling pace. Mentally and physically, I was in a place that I didn't want to be in. I wanted to get right back there, into the high, into nirvana where everything made sense. I wanted to go back there so I could take notes about all the amazing thoughts that had come into my head, the epiphanies I had had, the visions I had seen. The urge was too big. I lay down on the bed, hoping that the feeling would go away, that I would come to my senses and just leave. I tried to picture Tracy's face and the faces of my children. But the more I tried to distract myself, the stronger the urge got. *Eric,* I thought. *I need to find Eric. He needs to sort me out with another hit.*

I went downstairs to find him in his usual place, by the restrooms

"Hey man," I said, "have you got any more of that... stuff?"

He looked at me pensively.

"Oh yeah, you're ready to go again, big man?"

"Yeah, just one more time."

He scoffed.

"Alright, Freddie, you're my pal, I've got you. The first one was free, but I can't be handing out freebies every five minutes, you know, I'll go out of business."

"I've got money," I assured him. And it was true, I did. The fact that it was rent money didn't really bother me at the moment. All I could think of was going back upstairs and stepping on the rocket ship again.

Meanwhile, Tracy was at home with our two kids. When I still hadn't returned home late that evening, she called the hotel. But by then, I was too high to answer the phone. My body was lying flat on the hotel bed while my brain was out in space.

The next day, she called again and again. When I hadn't been in touch for a few days, she left the kids with a family member and came and saw me at the bar. I was working the early shift, knowing full well that if I were gonna get high again, I would need to earn money.

"Freddie, what the hell is going on?!" she asked. I took her aside.

"Tracy, you won't believe the trips I've had," I told her, my eyes big like saucers.

"Trips?"

"Don't get mad at me, but I tried crack. It's amazing. It will BLOW your mind…"

Tracy pushed my hands away and hissed:

"Crack?! Are you crazy?!"

"No, Tracy, don't judge me until you've tried it! I'm telling you, I'm a more knowledgeable person for having tried it."

"Freddie, we have KIDS!"

"I know… but please listen… I will be home later. We will talk then, OK?"

The truth was that I was feeling anxious, nauseated, and low. I was itching to get back up to the hotel room for another hit. As long as I stayed at the Globe, I had access to anything I needed. If I wanted a clean bed to sleep in, it was there for me. If I needed to smoke rock, it was available to me. If I needed some coke or other kind of drug to manage the comedowns, I had that too. Around the Globe, I was respected and loved. And my brain was screaming for me to smoke crack again, my thoughts were running crazy in my head, forming all sorts of arguments about why I needed the Globe and the drugs.

"Freddie…" she said with tears in her eyes. "I love you."

I looked at her, and I knew that I was breaking her heart. But the urge was too much for me, and I needed to take another hit.

"I love you too," I said, coldly. "See you later."

Days went past, maybe weeks. I lost track of time and space. I never had a clue of what day it was, and it didn't matter. If I was lying on the bed and I was needed in the bar, they would respectfully ask me to come down. I could work high, no problem, and I really needed to hold on to the job. It wasn't just the money, no, the Globe had become my sanctuary. And for the foreseeable future, it was also to become my family and home.

Sometimes, during my most excruciating lows and comedowns, I would call Tracy and tell her that I missed her and the kids, and that I loved them so, so much. Tracy would cry and say,

"But as long as you're smoking that shit, you're not coming home."

"Please, Tracy, can I at least see the kids? Just for an hour?"

She allowed me to come home and see our children, on one condition: I needed to be sober. I promised her that I would, but looking back, I know I was getting high every day because I felt that I couldn't live without the drugs. I'd go and see our children, stroke their beautiful faces, and watch them play. Then the urge to get high would grip me, and I made my excuses and left.

Finding truth was paramount to me, and that's what I thought I was doing while smoking rock. I had walked around with the feeling of being lied to and kept in the dark most of my life, and I wanted to break free from that. So, every day, I tried to chase that feeling again, the one I had felt doing crack for the first time. The comedowns got worse, but the high was never quiet was the same after that first time. Nothing could compare to it. Nothing even came close.

I had a better understanding of people now. I could finally understand why my sisters had done what they had done. They were all in search of something, and the drugs provided plenty of comfort. What my parents had said about drug users wasn't true. What they had said about bikers and Hells

Angels wasn't true. I still loved my parents to death, but I realized that they were the ones who were kept in the dark, not me. Understanding the world, the drug users, people who were different, made me into a better person. They weren't dangerous or disgraceful people; they were my friends.

Friends on drugs weren't the most trustworthy friends, however, as I learned along the way. A pal of mine came to stay in the room with me for a few nights. He was into crack and coke as well. After he had left, I was getting ready to cook some, when I realized that he had swapped my cocaine for baking soda!

Every so often, Tracy would call or come over to the bar to scream and cry.

"You're on this holiday while I work full time and look after our kids," she'd sob. And she was right, but I was already too deep. There wasn't much that was going to stop me now. That's what crack does, it convinces you that your relationship with the drug is the only one that matters. Fuck family, fuck friends.

"Why can't you just quit the drugs, come home and be with the kids and me?" she pleaded.

"I'm on a path. This is something I feel I need to do."

"I thought we were on a path together," she quietly sobbed.

"You walk your path but it's not for me. This is where I need to be now.

"But please, just try to quit! It's ruining you!"

"Hey, don't knock it 'til you try it!" I told her. She hung up on me.

She doesn't understand, I thought. *She just doesn't understand.*

The bar was my core. If I had the respect of the bar scene, I felt that was enough.

One day, Gary knocked on my door. He was the young man who had once given me crystal meth at a dinner party. Since then, we had occasionally smoked crack together. When I saw his face, I knew exactly what was up. He was sliding off his wig, aggressive and foaming at the mouth.

"Where is it? Have you got it?"

"What?"

"You took my fucking stuff!"

"What are you talking about?"

"Give me the crack!"

"Listen fucker, I haven't got your fucking crack. I bought my own!"

He lurched at me with long, dirty fingers that were clawing at my face like an Orc clawing at a hobbit. His eyes were oddly intense but empty at the same time. I had to fight him off me and push him into the corridor again. I quickly locked the door as he tumbled into the wall. But he didn't give up. He banged on the door and made gut-wrenching noises for what felt like an hour afterward. He had gone paranoid. It wasn't the first time I had seen that kind of behavior, but I had never been the victim of it like this before. I stopped doing drugs with people and decided to keep more to myself.

I became even more isolated after my fight with Gary. I realized that I couldn't trust anyone, not even other drug addicts, and the people who didn't do drugs would just judge me. I didn't want anyone around me now. The days were spent, chasing the experience of that first-ever hit. While I never reached it again, smoking still felt better than not smoking. It made me feel so sharp, so powerful, and that I could overcome anything. It was the only thing that mattered, and I was convinced I was doing myself a favor. My brain kept making up logical reasons as to why smoking crack made me more intelligent. I didn't need sleep. I didn't need food. I could just keep going and because of the drugs, my brain just kept telling me: "you don't need anything, you just need to get some more." The longest I could ever stay straight was around eight hours. I'd work a long shift, knowing that once I clocked out, I'd have enough money to buy another hit.

I owed it to the world to become this informed, knowledgeable person. Nothing else mattered. My mind was exploring all the sensations, wisdom, and knowledge. And I wasn't supposed to understand what day of the week it was. What did I give a shit, whether it was a Sunday or a Wednesday and what did it even matter?

Every night after my shift ended, I went to see Eric who would give me an ounce. It would get me through the night, and if I was lucky, I would get some sleep at around seven or eight o'clock in the morning. I would then sleep until noon, get up, get high, and try and keep my shit together before going down and doing another shift, making the money so that I would have another big bag to come "home" to. Then I would do it all over again.

It had been over six months since I first tried it, and I didn't even care to hide my addiction anymore. I just had to pace myself, so my eyeballs didn't resemble marshmallows bulging out of my head when I started my shift. By now, even some of the guys at the Globe were disappointed. Those boys that I respected, they weren't respecting me no more. They were really worried about me. A few of them would pull me aside and say "Fuck, Freddie, you're in fucking bad shape. Be careful, you're on a fucking slippery slope here."

I was not in contact with anybody outside of the bar community, people from the Globe, Queens, or Balmoral. And unless I was asking them for money, I was never speaking to my parents anymore. The money I made at the bar was just enough to get high every night. When I needed more and my dad said no, I stole from my own mother. She was working at a craft fair at the mall, so I walked there and grabbed the money from the till.

I was working my last hour on a late shift after closing, and my body was screaming for a high. I felt my heart palpitate and the anxiety rise, hoping that somehow the clock on the wall would start to race, and my shift would be over. Normally I would be binging on crack, chasing one high after another, and then finally doing a little bit of something else just to get me relaxed enough to sleep. I knew that I wasn't gonna be able to go to sleep that night without drugs. One of the guests, a friend of the owner, was muttering loudly while fiddling with something in the corner. *What the fuck is he doing*, I thought. It turned out he was making blotter acid. He was working with small pieces of paper, the ones with little blue squares on, and dropping acid into each square. Suddenly, he swore, and I saw that one of his squares had gotten wet from the beer spilled on the counter. He crumpled the little piece of paper, threw it on the floor, and mumbled "Fucking garbage!"

"No!" I winced. I couldn't stand seeing any kind of drug going to waste.

"Well, you can have it if you want," the man scoffed.

I picked it up from the dirty bar floor and put it in my mouth. The next thing I knew, I was on the phone to Tracy, telling her: "I think I'm gonna fucking die."

She came down and took me to the hospital. From the hospital. She took me to detox. Despite being mad at me, and not liking me much anymore, she still loved me. Tracy, the most beautiful lady, and best friend I could ask for, was always there for me, even at my lowest and even when I had betrayed her the most.

The detox centers were rough places. I came in straight from the emergency ward, and they strip-searched me and then let me lie in a bed in a room full of other beds. Around me were people just like me, some screaming in anguish, some deadly silent. There were nurses walking around, checking on us. But there were to be no drugs, no medicine to take the pain away.

Over eight months, Tracy ended up taking me to detox twice. And both times I swore to her that I would quit.

CHAPTER 6

Sinking Through the Floor

The day Jesse was born, I phoned my dad up from the hospital. I had just held my baby son in my arms for the first time when I had an epiphany. I said, "Dad, you know how you always ask me what I want to be? I have the answer for you now. I want to be a great dad. I just want to be a standup dad like you were. If anything, I want to be an even better dad. So that is my answer, I want to be a good father."

I had meant those words. Now, several months into my addiction, I was lying on my hotel bed, just high enough to get some sleep, when there was a knock on my door. "Go away!" I yelled at whoever was at the door.

"There's a phone call for you!" the voice said, "It's Tracy, and she sounds pretty worked up." My first instinct was to ignore it and go to sleep. But then it hit me that there might have been a serious accident and that's why she called. I eventually made it out of bed and downstairs to the phone. Tracy was crying.

"What's wrong?" I asked.

"I thought you would have called today."

"What?" There was a deep sigh on the other side of the line, then she was quiet for a bit, as if she was trying to keep herself together.

"I take it there isn't a card coming in the post any time soon, huh?"

"What are you talking about?"

"Have you forgotten what day it is?" she snapped.

I didn't even know what month it was. But I knew the nature of these calls. A few months earlier, I had missed my parents' anniversary. I had gotten a disappointed phone call the day after. It could have been Valentine's Day, my birthday or even Canada Day for all I knew. But neither of us had the energy or time for guessing games. From out of nowhere, I had a flashback from the previous week, when I had spent the money meant for a toy truck for Jesse on cocaine.

"Jesse..." I said.

"Yep. He's going to bed in a minute. Care to say happy birthday?"

"Yeah, put him on!"

I had missed my son's third birthday. My heart sank down into my stomach and out of my ass. For the first time in months, I felt something other than the urge. I felt profound shame and guilt.

There was a crackling noise, and then I heard his sweet voice on the phone. I dried my tears, and I promised him I'd go and see him the following week. Hopefully, I would get paid before then, and be able to pick up a toy from some-where before then.

"On Friday, when mommy's working, I'm coming to look after you and Jaz," I said.

Taking me to detox had not helped. When Tracy had picked me up, I had cried and promised her I'd quit. I wanted to go home and be with her and the kids. But as soon as I had come out, I had fallen right back into the darkness again. And so it went, I took drugs and forgot to eat. When I was on the verge of disappearing, Tracy would come and pick me up, call me a skeleton, and I'd promise her this was the last time.

Before we hung up the phone, I talked to her and arranged to come and watch the kids while she was working a late shift.

"Just promise me, Freddie, no drugs in the house. It's just for six hours. OK?"

"I promise. I can't wait to see the kids," I said and meant every word of it.

Once we had said our goodbyes, I went upstairs to bed and forgot all about them again. My high had been ruined, and all I wanted to do was to go on that magic carpet ride and forget all my guilt. Smoking crack was like putting on a safety cloak. It would immediately fix whatever was wrong. If I were sad, I'd smoke, and I'd be happy. It didn't matter that my hair needed washing, I smelled like a dumpster truck, and my bones were visible through my skin. Drugs made everything better.

Friday came, and I shakily put my clothes on to go home. I had mixed feelings about it, a part of me missed the kids something crazy, but a different part of me wanted to stay back at the hotel and smoke. I took one last look in the mirror before I set off. I could barely recognize myself anymore. The person staring back at me was pale and bony, with dark circles under his eyes. I closed my eyes and said a little prayer that I wouldn't scare the kids off, coming home looking like the boogeyman.

But the kids weren't scared. They welcomed me home with their little smiley faces and soft, sticky hands. Tracy came out from the bedroom, clipping a pair of golden earrings onto her earlobes. She looked beautiful.

"I'm leaving now," she said. "Please call me if you need anything. And..." she lowered her voice. "Please remember what we agreed on?"

"Of course!" I exclaimed. "I won't let you down. I love you."

"I love you too," she said and left.

We spent most of the evening reading books and watching video tapes. As the hours went past, I felt more and more desperate. Finally, it was bedtime for the kids. I brushed their teeth with shaky hands and got them into their pyjamas. When I thought they were both sound asleep I went around the apartment, looking for drugs. I had been over a few times per month to see them, and I had hidden coke in various places, should I ever get desperate. I went into the kitchen and checked the air vent, and sure enough, I had taped a little piece to it. I ended up smoking it in the house, sitting on the kitchen floor. I was far away in space, so I didn't hear the little footsteps coming around the corner.

Jesse stopped in his tracks right in front of me. Our eyes locked. I looked into his big eyes, his innocent, curious face, and I didn't see my son. I saw myself as a little boy.

As a child, my father was my hero. He didn't often lecture or preach, he led by doing, and I learned by watching. Every summer, he'd take me fishing by the Skeena River. He'd dip his hand in the water as if he was trying to catch it, and he'd say, "Look, Freddie, the water always finds a way." I knew what he meant, what he wanted to say: that I could do anything and that I was like water, impossible to stop. Even logs and rocks couldn't stop the water, it was gonna continue to go sideways and eventually get back onto its own path again.

That was my dad, always wanting me to think my way out of things and always wanting me to know that there were solutions to most things. You just had to create them within yourself and never give up. You had to make a move, even if it was the wrong move, because you'd learn from it. You could turn left and go the wrong way, but at least you wouldn't be standing in the fucking intersection waiting to get hit. Once you had turned left, you could just go back and go right, and if it ended up being the right path, then away you go, but don't stand still. You always get up; you always get moving. You always overcome. That was his mantra and the words he wanted me to remember.

My dad had an amazing and spiritual relationship with nature. He even seemed to have the ability to communicate with animals. He just got them so well. When we were camping, he'd call out to a loon, and the loon would call back. I could tell that his respect for the First Nations community was huge. He'd teach me about their spirit animals, especially the Kermode bear, and I loved listening to him talk. The ancient legend told of a raven who had once created the world. When the raven transformed the earth from cold and icy to warm and green, it turned every tenth black bear white to remind people of the frozen world they had once lived in. The ghost bears were the spirits of the rainforests, and they could swim deep underwater and lead people to magical places.

When I got a little bit older, Dad would take me moose hunting, teaching me the ways of the animal. We'd board the boat on the Babine Lake in Northern BC, and the shore would smell of rotting fish. Once out on the river, the smell was long gone, and instead, I could enjoy the gentle laps of the water, and watch my dad watching the shoreline. "You need to follow the fog, Freddie," he'd say with his back turned to me, "watch it rolling and lifting." I watched it. He understood the moose so well, how it would hide from danger but still stay on the edge. We kept the motor off, not to scare away the animals, and we'd just be floating on the river, quietly bobbing up and down until we lost movement, and then we'd paddle around the creek. He'd stop paddling and take his gun out. Just as we turned the corner, the fog would be lifting, and there, a tall, majestic moose stood every time. Two shots and it was down. The moose didn't just feed our family but loads of families on our street. It hung in our garage for days. I'd watch dad carve out and hand out ribs, and it was beautiful to see the whole process in its entirety. Although I had been scared the first time he'd taken me out shooting, I now saw what all that was for. He had taught me the circle of life.

My dad always wanted to do things by the book, even if it took longer and was harder. He'd turn off the boat's motor if the law said so. Doing drugs was bad because the law said so. Since my teenage years, I had thought of him as naive, but now I could appreciate him for always trying to be an upstanding citizen, even if he occasionally got it wrong, or if our opinions differed. He was a hard-working man, always getting up at dawn and not coming home until the late evening. He would spend the weekends with me, and he'd make them the best weekends a boy could ever hope for. It wasn't fair for me to judge him, especially after learning about his background.

My father had been born to a prostitute addicted to drugs. He would leave out the details when talking about his mother, but nothing he had to say about her was pretty. His parents couldn't care for him or his sister, so by the time he was 14, he had left home to become a welder. It wasn't until many years later that his grandmother called and said that someone was looking for him.

"There is an advert in the paper and they're looking for a Sonny Karlsson, born February 12th, 1933."

"And?"

"That's you," she said.

It transpired that his mother had married a Swedish sailor named Karlsson and he was my dad's real father. When dad was two years old, they had separated but never divorced. The Swede had sailed back to Sweden, and his mother had buried the papers and later remarried a man called Tom Wilson. Then, they re-named my dad too. The newspaper advert had been put out as the Swede, my real grandfather, had died, and his family wanted to alert my dad. "After all these years," they had said, "your dad really wanted you to know the truth."

When my dad met my mom, she had recently gotten out of an abusive marriage. She had three little girls, but it never put my dad off. He fell in love with her and promised to raise the kids as his own.

He was a good man and a fantastic father to all of us. And while sitting on Tracy's kitchen floor, I realized that my dad was put on this earth just to be my dad. That's all he ever wanted. He just wanted to have time with me. And the only thing I wanted was to be Jesse's and Jaz's dad.

I had been so happy as a child, so proud of my family, and so content with my life. I had been the golden boy like Jesse was now. It was easier to see now that I was high, because my mind was clearer. I was looking at the child who had had everything and then had everything taken away from him. I was failing this beautiful, perfect little boy. I was jeopardizing my whole life and a chance to be his and Jaz's father, which wasn't right.

I kept thinking, what if it were my dad? What I was doing was so much worse than my parents had done to me. I was killing myself with the drugs and therefore letting my children and my wife down. It got too much for me, and I started to cry. I don't know how long I sat there, crying. But this time, I decided that I needed to quit, for real. I needed this to stop, and I needed to be the dad I had once promised myself I would be.

But I knew I couldn't quit forever. I had tried twice before by saying, "I'm gonna quit, and I'm gonna quit forever, and I'm never gonna fucking do this." I knew that I needed to raise Jesse to an age where I could sit down and discuss doing crack and possibly do it with him as messed up as that might sound. That's what I was thinking. And that I had to raise him to be able to explain everything to him. I had to tell him my story so that he could understand. If he ever started smoking crack, I didn't want him to do it unprepared. The drugs were still manipulating my mind, and instead of thinking that I didn't want him ever to try it, I wanted him to try it while having an understanding of it first. So, while I thought I couldn't get off the drugs forever, I had to pause it for thirteen years until Jesse was old enough to understand and make his own decisions.

I can't remember if I walked home that night or if Tracy gave me a ride home. But later, I called her up and told her: "I'm quitting this shit. I'm going straight for you and the kids."

She sighed and said, "I don't believe you."

"I mean it this time."

We hung up. I left the hotel. I took a taxi to the detox center. I was going to go clean for good this time, I thought. But the staff recognized me.

"This is your third time coming here," they said. "You're not serious about quitting, so we can't help you."

And with those words, they sent me away.

Back at the hotel, I was pacing back and forth. I was going to get through this. I was going to go clean. All I needed to do was to get through the night. I lay down in bed, trying to get a wink, but my mind was racing, and my heart was thumping. I looked at the clock on the wall. It was just after midnight. At 9 am, I was going to make some phone calls and make sure I got the help I needed. Everything was going to be fine, I thought, I just needed to make it until 9 am. When I glanced at the clock again, it was still just a few minutes past midnight. Time stood still. I felt something like cockroaches crawling under my skin, and I got up and started pacing around the room. I knew Eric wasn't at the hotel at the moment, so even if I wanted some, I couldn't get it. I started to panic. It was only 1 am, and I was never going to be able to sleep without getting high. *Maybe I hid some in my room when I was really high?* I wondered. So, with shaky hands, I started to tear open drawers, turn over chairs, and snatch clothes out of the closet. I was going skitzy, with my hands and knees on the carpet, looking for any specs of white that I could have dropped. I just needed a little bit, just a tiny bit to get me through the night. And I ended up busting open the glass pipes, lying on the floor. There was even a light bulb that I had used at one point to smoke crystal meth. I broke them all up and scraped the residue out and smoked it. It was dirty, old residue from months gone by. Pure filth. I did not have a good reaction to it.

I started to feel hot. Soon I was scorching. Like drenched in lava, burning from the inside kind of hot. Sweat was pouring down my temples, and I got up from the floor and started tearing off my clothes. I got into the bathroom, and all I could think was, *if I don't cool down, I'm gonna die.*

Naked, I got into the shower, and I grabbed the shower hose, supporting my weight with one hand on the wall. The cold water felt good. I stood like that for a long time, gradually cooling down, listening to the gentle splashes. I was staring at my feet and the water going down the drain the whole time, fixating on the small, square holes in an attempt to stay conscious. Suddenly, I saw something under the drain move. It appeared to be crawling up and out. I kept staring at it. It looked like a moth, so white it was nearly translucent. The thing slowly grew closer until it wrapped itself around my feet and ankles and proceeded to wrap itself around my knees and torso until I was completely gone.

CHAPTER 7

Refuge

The overdose was painless, I merely dissipated. The moth had swallowed me whole and re-birthed me in the form of its offspring. It was as if I were a moth too, and I was swarming over my human body that was lying on the bathroom floor. I looked at it, thinking, *it is not supposed to be there. But then again, I'm not really here either.*

The swarming and buzzing gently faded, and suddenly I was sitting in lotus position in a room that felt familiar to me. Somehow, I knew it as *the book writing room*. I could hear voices, but I couldn't see anyone. I was in a crowded hall, but I was still all alone. This was the room where the story of your life was written. I was writing my own book, but when I went to turn the page, I saw that it was the last one. I was running out of pages. I was running out of time. *I can't be here.* I heard myself say. *I need one more chance, please just gimme one more chance.* I could feel them all around me, the people, the swarm of moths fluttering around the room. *This isn't how we wrote the book; this isn't supposed to be my story. Let me go back to try and finish my story. I do not wanna be here. Please let me have one more chance.* I felt a warm presence and then silence.

I woke up on the bathroom floor with Eric dragging me by my hair into the living room. And that's when he grabbed me, looked down at me, and said, "This fucking shit is not going to kill you. *I'm* gonna fucking kill you. I'm gonna fucking do it right now." And he hit his fist so hard right beside my head that he put a hole in the floor.

I was so scared I couldn't speak. It was like he had pulled me up from under the surface just as I was about to fall asleep, submerged with water. I was still hallucinating, and his red face looked like something out of a horror movie. He pulled his fist back up, and he was just absolutely shaking with rage. He looked like he was going to punch me in the face, but instead, he said, "Fuck, I'll give you one more chance! You get the fuck outta here. If I ever fucking see you again, if you're ever in this fucking place or anywhere around here, I'll fucking kill you." His breath was hot and rancid. He leaned even closer to my face and hissed through gritted teeth, "Get your fucking clothes and get the fuck outta here."

Confused and still in a haze, I got my clothes from the floor and started dressing. Eric left the room but came back a few minutes later. He seemed to have calmed down a notch but was still angry. He handed me a bag of weed and said, "Here, you'll need this." Then he watched as I grabbed my bag and left. "Don't let me catch you around here again!" I heard him call after me as I tumbled down the stairs.

I stumbled out of the hotel. I couldn't go home; the kids couldn't see me overdosing like this. I needed to get far, far from the Globe, the bar community in Nanaimo, and the drugs. I knew what I had done, it was serious. There was no turning back from this. Yes, I could have died, but that wasn't the reason Eric was livid with me. Overdosing was the biggest betrayal. If he hadn't pulled me out of the shower and a cleaning lady had found me like that the next morning instead, it would have been the end of me and the end of them. If I had died, I would have gotten everyone in trouble. Eric could have gone to jail. I understood the implications of my actions. I needed to go before someone found out and came after me.

Somehow, I got to a phone, and I dialed a number I hadn't dialed in a very long time. The phone rang for what felt like an eternity until there was a click when the person on the other side of the line picked up the receiver.

"Hello?"

Her sweet voice was like honey to my ears. It was my big sister Ramona, one of the few people in my family who could fully relate to what I was going through. She lived in Vancouver, a ferry ride away. Kindly, she invited me to stay with her until I was back on my feet.

Vancouver was the ideal place for me to disappear to. I didn't know anyone around there, no one could find me and get me into trouble. I had to isolate myself from anybody that had any knowledge of where to get drugs.

When I arrived, she welcomed me with a hug. She was just as beautiful as she had been as a teenager. Her house was homely and inviting, a far cry from the trailer she had lived in a decade earlier. There were pictures of her family on the wall. The wholesome faces and bright smiles in the portraits gave no hint of Ramona's messy past. It made me feel as if I had dreamt it all. I stopped for a moment to take it all in, the smell of the home-cooked food, the everyday family life she now seemed to live. She gave me a tour of the house and then showed me where I was gonna sleep.

When she was 17, Ramona had Aaron, her first son. Becoming a mother gave her the motivation to go clean. Now she was giving me a chance to do the same. The first two weeks spent at her house were horrendous. My whole body ached and was at war with my brain. My still-addicted brain kept trying to convince me to go out and find crack. Luckily for me, that option wasn't there anymore. So, I spent two weeks just resting and recovering from the overdose. I slept in my clothes and boots, got up in the mornings and ate a bowl of cereal, smoked some weed with my headphones on, and went back to bed. I just slept and slept. My body needed it after nearly a year of abuse.

I called Tracy every night. She cried and asked why I couldn't come home and be with them. I told her that I was better off away from them so that I could come home when I was completely clean, and we could start over. I promised her that, and every day I longed for my family, to see Tracy and touch her again, be her husband again, and be a dad to my kids. But going home was risky. By overdosing at the hotel, I made a lot of enemies. Still, nothing would have kept me from going back there, trying to score. The drugs still had me in their chokehold because that is just how drugs work.

I spent a lot of time thinking back on my time as a substance abuser. How it had all happened by chance, that one time when Eric made me do it. My whole life, I had been told that drugs were bad, with no nuance or truth offered, just a black-and-white statement. They were bad and taken by bad people. If you did drugs, you too would become bad. I understood why my parents had told me that. My father grew up with a drug addict, and my mother watched her three daughters become addicted to drugs at an early age. But they were never honest about how the substance made you feel things you could never feel in any other situation. They never told me how it opens your mind and makes you think clearly. They never mentioned the new perspectives the drugs would offer or how it felt like a warm hug from someone you loved when you were at your lowest point. Maybe I felt lied to, and when I first smoked crack with Eric, I felt like I had made an amazing discovery. Out of all drugs out there, crack is one of the most addictive. Being on it feels like being involved in a passionate but toxic love affair. Drugs manipulate you to think that you depend on them, that doing them is doing yourself a favor. It will tell you that you are becoming a more knowledgeable and honorable person. The first time you try crack is the most amazing feeling in the world. Nothing can beat it. Literally. Because you will never be able to feel that way again, but you will continue to try. So, throughout your addiction, you will chase a high you will never reach again. Sometimes you may get close, but your body has built up immunity not to allow it. And one day, you wake up, and it's been a year.

Maybe if I had a more nuanced description of what it was like, I wouldn't have gotten so swept away. Maybe if someone had sat me down and explained how the brain acted on drugs and explained why it felt so good, I would have had a better understanding, and I would have been able to make better choices.

I thought about how my other sister Deanna had also been addicted to drugs and then come off them when she married the police officer. She hadn't spoken about it; it was almost like it was a big secret. I knew there and then that one day, I would be on the other side. Right now, I was recovering from an overdose, I was wearing the same stinking clothes I had worn for a week. I was skinny, weak, and emotionally fragile. But given time, I would be strong, work a good job, and be a great father and husband again. Then I would tell people my story, and I would spend my time helping others who were recovering. If I could stay alive for these few months, I could go out into the world and do great things. I could write my story, and it wouldn't end with me dying on a wet and dirty bathroom floor or even with me riding off into the sunset, clean as a whistle. I would write my story, and it would involve helping others and spreading awareness about drugs. No scaremongering or propaganda, only the truth.

I spent the first two weeks at Ramona's in turmoil. It was as if I had walked through a door and fallen into a great black hole of nothingness, and I couldn't stop falling. Whenever Ramona or anyone from her family tried to talk to me, they mainly got grunts in return. My brain was constantly playing tricks on me, trying to justify drug use. Quitting crack was like quitting a part of myself. It felt like giving up all the things that were good in my life. It was like having to take the bus to school after riding a Cadillac for a year. I had been flying with the gods, and now I was walking the streets with demons. I was fighting a war with myself, the bloodiest, most gruesome battle, and I had lost some limbs. Or that is what it felt like, anyway.

I went between having sleepless nights where the urge to do crack was so strong, that it was eating me alive, to sleeping for days while having strange and vivid dreams. I would close my eyes and feel my body getting sucked into a drain. Demons chased me and tried to claw my eyes out, screaming that I was a lousy father, a shitty husband, a shitty son. Sometimes I was in a car that would suddenly catch fire. When I tried to get out, the doors were locked. I'd scream. And then I'd see the people. Just silhouettes of people; adults and children, and I didn't know if they were strangers or my friends and family. But they were coming closer, surrounding the car, and instead of helping me, they threw gasoline onto the flames. *You piece of shit,* they screamed at me, *you're going to fucking die.* And I'd be pounding on the windows, shouting *But I'm not a bad person,* to no avail. The dreams could last for hours, or they could last a few minutes, but I always woke up, drenched in my own sweat, shaking.

After the initial two weeks, the dreams became less frequent, less intense. It was not as if someone had flipped a switch, the change was subtle. It gave me a chance to breathe, and to attempt to look into the future to see what it could hold. I was out of the hotel; I was away from Eric and the drugs. I was with family. Now I knew that I was on a path and that I had a big job ahead of me. I had to prove to my wife that I could do this. I had to prove to my parents that I could do this. But to be able to get back on my feet, I needed money and something to do. I needed a job.

CHAPTER 8

Swimming Upstream

The Canadian Superstore needed workers for their night shifts, and I needed something to get me through the sleepless nights and bad dreams. I was stocking shelves for $6.30 an hour from midnight onwards. I hated the job at first. It was monotonous and hard, and I was struggling with feelings of depression and anger. I hated feeling like such an unsuccessful piece of shit, to going from being the king of the hill at the Globe to shelving groceries in a cold warehouse, but I told myself that at least I was alive and working on getting my life back together. When I called Tracy to tell her I got the job, she cried tears of happiness. I said: "You know what? This is a shitty job, but it's just gonna get me through until I'll be able to find something that's gonna be enough to give you and the kids the lifestyle you deserve."

"Does this mean you won't come home?" she cried. "I wanna see you. I miss you."

I knew she didn't trust me enough to come home and live with her again, but I vowed to come home and see them on the days I didn't work. Tracy wanted to support me fully through my recovery journey, and we were determined to get through it together.

As soon as our children were asleep, she called me, and we talked for hours. We were slowly building trust. In a way, it was like our relationship started over, and we were courting again. This time, we had two children, but the feeling of falling in love again was still magical. Not much else feels magical when you try to beat your drug addiction. Most things feel bleak and dull.

When I next saw Tracy, I made a deal with her. "I'll make a million dollars, and I won't drink or touch anything other than pot until I've raised the kids." And as soon as I made the deal with her, she knew I was gonna come through with it.

My supervisor saw that I had some aggression in me and muscles from playing hockey and got me cutting stock. When the pallets of stock came in, and they were huge, two guys in front of me would put the box of pickles on the floor, right in front of the pickle shelf. Then I would run in behind them, and I would cut that box open, and I would put the pickles on the shelf, and move on to the next case they had on the floor. I did it because I hated the job so much, I just wanted to get it done and get out of there. My supervisor thought he'd make use of my pent-up aggression and said: "Hey Wilson, if you can cut stock faster than those two can throw it on the floor in front of you, you are welcome to kick both of their asses."

I didn't have anything better to do, so I started chasing these guys around, shouting, "Am I gonna catch you? Better run, or I'll kick your asses!"

Well fuck, we stocked half the store, three of us, a job that usually took twelve men. I would chase the poor fuckers three nights a week, and then on the four days I had off, I would take the sky train and the ferry to see Tracy.

During this time, I was often reminded of the Koi fish. I had first heard the story a few years back while getting a tattoo at the Dutchman. This guy had come out of the studio with a brand-new Chinese-looking fish tattooed on his arm, and after he had left, I asked my tattooist what the deal with the fish was. He had told me about the Chinese Koi fish waterfall legend.

Long ago, the Yellow River in China had been agleam with the golden Koi fish. They were different from most other fish because they built strength and perseverance through swimming upstream and going against the current. Through always swimming upstream, the fish became braver and took on more daring challenges until they tried to swim up the most dizzying waterfall known as the Dragon's Gate in Hunan province. Not only did the fish have to deal with an impossible waterfall, but there were also fishermen who tried to get them. Here, most of the fish gave up and swam back down, while only the most dedicated koi kept pursuing the waterfall. Although they tried for a hundred years, they couldn't get over that one impossible obstacle, and the river's spirits watched, amused when the koi failed over and over again.

Finally, once a hundred years had passed, one koi thought to try something different. It turned back and swam towards the bottom of the river, convincing everyone that it had given up. But then it turned around and swam upwards again, this time building speed. It swam and swam and finally leaped out of the water and reached the mountain's top. There, the fish found the most tranquil pond to finally rest in. The spirits had never seen anyone defeat the waters like that, and as a reward, they transformed this one koi into a golden dragon. After all the hard work, the fish had turned into the ultimate symbol of strength and courage, and now he was getting his revenge on the fishermen and everyone who tried to fight him as he had tried to reach his goals.

Working at the superstore, I felt like that koi. The addiction to drugs and alcohol was a huge obstacle to overcome. It was like swimming upstream in an impossible waterfall. I had so much frustration and anger that I was dealing with I didn't give a shit what was in my way up that fucking waterfall. And that was my attitude in the Superstore. I didn't take any shit from anybody. I got into fights with the district manager and ripped him right in front of the whole crew. Then the store manager would come in and talk to me in an intimidating way. I just looked at him and scoffed, "Fuck off, buddy. You can't talk professionally to me? You must try and intimidate me with this bullshit fucking voice?"

He grinned his ugly grin. "Do you want me to talk in a baby voice to you?" he mocked.

I had no patience anymore. I wasn't going to take bullshit from people in powerful positions. There were all these managers who didn't know how to manage, and they were just kicking the shit out of their people. Somehow, I managed to get the right people on my side. Maybe because I was really good at it and despite not taking any shit, the managers liked me. Climbing the mountain upstream seemed to finally pay off. I was even offered a full-time job there. But I couldn't accept it, as I needed to go back to Vancouver Island more often. I was rebuilding my relationship with my wife and my kids. That was my main goal, and I wasn't gonna give that up. Tracy was slowly trusting me and taking me in. She often reminded me that she was proud of me, and I wasn't gonna fuck that up.

Once as I was clocking off for the week, my supervisor asked me, "Why do you keep going to the Island? Why don't you transfer to Duncan? They're not doing too good and need a full-timer."

So, I said I'd be happy to. Tracy saw that I was being genuine this time around and that I was keen to build us a new life. When I proposed the move to Duncan, she happily agreed, and we rented a place out there. It was ideal for us to finally be living together again, far away from anyone who might recognize me or offer me drugs.

But the store was just as bad as my supervisor had said. It was a fairly new store, and the shelves were almost empty. They ended up firing the store manager for poor management. One day, the district manager came in and ordered half of all staff to come in and fill the shelves. Now, we were normally going through five hundred to six hundred cases per shift, about a trailer load. On this day, 3,000 cases were waiting for us, three or four trailer loads of stock. We pulled it off the trailers, we hit the floor, we actually cut it all, but just barely. We came in the next night, and there were another fucking 3,000 pieces waiting for us. We bust our asses again, and we got all the stock cut before opening time, except for some cardboard in the meat department. Customers were coming in, and we were still cleaning up the few pieces of cardboard. The district manager blew up. He ordered all of us into the back room and started ripping us.

"You're not doing your fucking jobs!" he shouted, red in the face. "And because of you lazy bastards, the store manager had to lose his job, and if you think you can stand a chance in this store, you better fucking pull your pants up and work!"

I was standing in the back, getting increasingly furious with this guy but dedicatedly biting my tongue. It was as if he could see the fury seeping out of my pores, however, and he looked at me and said, "You got something to say?"

"Yeah, I've got something to say," I hissed. "You think that any of us are gonna fucking respect you after this? We do 500 or 600 pieces a night. You ordered fucking 3,000. We bust our asses to fucking get it done. The next day we've got 3,200. We get it done with a fucking little bit of cardboard in the fucking meat department. And you're telling us that we can't do our jobs and it was our fucking fault that the manager got fired." I stared him down, sick of his bullshit. I said, "I don't know how many fucking pieces you got coming in tonight, but you better be here with a fucking knife in your hand, helping us out because I ain't fucking busting my ass. And none of these guys busted their asses just to get fucking spoken to like this by you."

He just stared at me. Then he opened his mouth and bellowed, "Everybody outta here except for you." The other guys left the room, and I was standing opposite this man, wondering what the hell he was planning for me. What he did surprised me. He put his arm around me and said, "Very few people have ever talked to me like that. I'm not too happy with it. But..." he said, "I know those fucking guys on that crew are gonna respect you. What's your story?"

I told him I was a crack addict, trying to get my shit together for the kids.

"How about I put you on the promotion ladder?" He said, "You climb it as high as you want, you get off it whenever you want, and you can get a career with us."

That sounded good to me, so I agreed. It was no longer a job; it was a career. They tested me out for a few nights with me running the crew. And then the store manager came in and gave me the grocery manager job. Now I had a good salary, benefits, and bonuses. Respect was coming back. I got to promote people and change their lives for the better. It felt great.

There were district managers and people within the company who didn't want me to tell my story to others, but I did anyway. I told people I used to be a crackhead but had started working there to get my life in order to be able to raise my kids, and that at first, I hated it and used to try to beat my colleagues up. And once I would open up with people, I found that not only did they wanna work better, but they also wanted to work closer with me. And they also started to share their stories. When we started opening up about who we really were, we felt more welcome and successful for being there.

I worked as a grocery manager for eight months, and my colleagues and I did such a phenomenal job that we'd stand at the end of the aisles with our arms crossed, all proud, just admiring how nice and tidy it all was. When my manager, who was normally a cold-hearted bastard, came by, he walked up to me and said, "I don't want you to come in tonight. I want you to come in tomorrow morning instead." Then he asked,

"Have you got any tattoos on your ears and your neck?"

"No"

"Okay, in that case, get a haircut, put on a shirt and tie, and meet me here tomorrow morning. You're training with me as my assistant."

Another year after that, I was a store manager, making $150,000 a year. I had 250 people working for me. I had a secretary, three assistant managers, and 25 department managers, and the head office to deal with. Things were going great.

At home, Tracy had a full house. When the conversation eventually came to, 'should we have more kids or not', we both thought we were finished.

"Why don't you just get snipped?" Tracy suggested. I tried. I went to the doctor, who told me I was too young to have the procedure. I went back home and told Tracy, who said, "Ok, then I'll go and get my tubes tied." But there was a six-month waiting list. So, we waited six months, and when it was finally time for her to attend her appointment, they made an interesting discovery. She returned home and said, "It turns out they're not doing it now."

"Why not?" I asked, perplexed. "What is it with these doctors?"

"Well, they said they wouldn't do it as I'm pregnant."

I chuckled, putting it down to being a joke. Later, she asked me, "So, should we tell the kids?"

"Tell the kids what?"

"That they're having a little brother or sister?"

"Holy shit. You're serious!"

Eight months later, we had our third child, Dakota, who we usually call Peeky.

The company ended up doing a major renovation under my leadership, which really impressed the people above me. We had gone from 100,000 to 150,000 square feet with positive sales. Someone from the head office ended up flying out and doing an interview with me about the store. "This is amazing," he said, "How did you manage it?" I blushed when my team said it was my motivation and my team building that had made it happen. Later, the head office contacted me and said, "We want you to go to Fort McMurray to be the store manager there."

Why do they want me to go to the asshole of Canada, I thought. Uprooting the family again and moving to the tar sands was not exactly on my bucket list, but they gave me an offer that was hard to refuse. They needed me to stay there for about two years, and they would double my bonus, give me a huge salary increase, and sell our house for us. The whole family had a meeting where we voted about who wanted to go to Fort Mac and who wanted us to stay put. When Tracy asked, "Who wants to move to Fort Mac?" all hands went up. Without much further ado, we packed our suitcases.

I wasn't very successful for the first six months, but for the remainder of it, I managed to turn it all around, and the store made a great profit. It went from losing 750,000 dollars a year to being profitable by $1.2 – $1.3 million within the first year. I put different things in place that worked well for that kind of environment. But at that two-year mark, we felt that we had had enough of the tar sands, so I let the head office know that I was ready to go elsewhere. They got back to me saying that they needed me in one of the stores in Whitehorse, an area best described as the polar opposite of Fort McMurray! When I told the kids, they jumped with glee.

We ended up staying in Whitehorse for nearly ten years. It was an ideal place to raise the kids, with its beautiful wildlife and historic sites. What I really loved about the Yukon area is there were no false faces. Everybody was just being who they were. I believe that when we get into some big cities, a lot of people are just trying to put on a fake face to be like the Joneses but are really, deep inside, crazier than a fucking bat shit. But here, there were no false faces, nobody desperate to live behind a facade to keep up appearances. You'd have the mayor walking down the sidewalk to see Bobby passed out with a needle in his hand on the sidewalk and the mayor would just go, "Good morning, Bobby, how are you?"

It was very good for me. I find that everybody just fucking clams up as if nobody wants to talk about our reality. And there's so much ignorance and fear about it because of that. But here, nobody was judging you for having lived through hard times and addiction. No one raised an eyebrow if they saw you smoking a joint; they just couldn't give a rat's ass. There were huge drug problems and huge alcohol problems, but the stigma and judgment were luckily missing.

Some of my good friends up there would do drugs. They wouldn't really hide it from me, but they didn't openly do anything in front of me either, out of respect. They weren't the most upstanding citizens, but they were my friends, and to me, they were beautiful.

I caught my friend Kevin doing a line once, and everyone was mad at him that I saw it. Kevin felt genuinely upset that he had let me see it, but I told him: "This needs to stop here. You can do whatever you want. The only thing that's going to make me uncomfortable is thinking that you guys have to hide something from me. If you guys think I don't know you are doing this, fuck, I couldn't care less. I prefer to be around you guys when you're happy, open, and loving. And that's what you guys are like. The stuff isn't controlling your life as it did with me. You live a normal life. I wish I could live like you..."

That was probably the only time I had a conversation that frank with my friends up in Yukon.

I have been working with 250, even 300 people in six different stores. I always welcome these kinds of conversations, even when it's with people I work with. From a few chats I have had with staff, I have sometimes found out about their addictions. They were doing heroin or crack at the time but were still functioning as people and had functioning lives and jobs. When I opened up to them about my past struggles with addiction, and we had that talk where we swapped stories, they got a different perspective of it, as did I.

There was a man called Lloyd, who I worked with at one of the stores. He was deep in the shit with heroin back then. He approached me to say, "I really appreciate the little bits you've shared with me. Can we talk more?" I don't know what I said to him, but he got his life back on track after that. Five years later, he's married, he's got a successful company, and a beautiful character home in Nanaimo. He's the dragon of the legend of the koi fish. He's going after it, and he's going after it hard. I love that.

When I first stepped foot in the Superstore, I had come in with an attitude that still stuck many years on. I was still all about the people trying to overcome their obstacles. I still didn't accept poor management or injustice. So, I would go after head office; if they were being assholes, I'd go after department managers who used intimidation styles. You don't beat up your own people. You're only as good as your people. You treat them with respect. That is still my mantra.

CHAPTER 9

Brian, Crystal, and all the Others

The new house was like a dream to us. It was a resort with a lake, a 4,200 square-foot waterfront home with six bedrooms, about forty minutes south of Whitehorse. The kitchen was an old trackers cabin from a hundred years ago. A huge three-floor monstrous house was built onto the side of it, with a basement, living room, master bedrooms, and a whole upstairs floor of bedrooms. It was a bigger house than we needed, with seemingly endless space, but we knew we wanted to buy it.

We hadn't lived there long when one of our neighbors came by to say hello and introduce herself. She asked us if we wouldn't mind getting approved by the ministry of social services.

"How so?" I asked.

"I've got nine foster kids," she said. "And I would love to have a neighbor that's approved to be able to get the kids from the school bus or if I'm late or something… so they can come and hang out at your guys' house."

Tracy and I looked at each other. The Yukon territory had a lot of issues with homeless children, kids born with Fetal Alcohol Syndrome, and other children in need of extra support. We were definitely within our means to lend a helping hand!

A lady from the social services came by our house to interview us. I didn't go into detail about my past as a crack addict, I just told her that I had had some personal problems in the past, but that I had been completely sober for 20 years. As soon as the results came back in and we were cleared, the authorities approached us and asked if we wanted to take some foster children in. There were so many kids that needed a home and not enough families who could host them. It would only be for a while, until they could be placed with a safe family member.

This was a different ball game altogether. I was working long hours, and I thought that Tracy already had her hands full with our kids. But she sat me down and said that this was something we could do. We had been so lucky in life. I had been given a second chance, and now we all lived in our dream house. Why should we not give these children an opportunity?

Siblings Darian, seven, and Alora, two, needed a new home. I had seen a picture of the apartment they lived in, and it reminded me of my old hotel room at the Globe. Their parents were drug addicts, and they needed to get the hell out of it. So, we took them in.

Caring for Darian and Alora was an eye-opening experience. I taught them the things my dad had taught me and the things I had taught my children. They stayed with us for quite a while until their grandmother was able to take them in. But they would still come over and spend the weekends with us. One weekend, we were sitting around the dinner table, and Darian was teaching me the native tongue.

"And this is the word for 'fish'," he said, and let out a few vocals that I tried to copy.

"That's really good, Darian!" I said. "Who taught you all this?"

"The carver!"

"The carver?"

"He's this guy who comes to my school, and he teaches us how to carve, but he's also teaching us native tongue." And I said, "What's his name?"

"Brian."

"Brian?" I asked, and my mind started to wander.

—

I had been in the Whitehorse store for a couple of weeks when I first met Brian. He was a young man, just turned 18, First Nations, and with a mouth full of fangs. It all started when a woman came into the store and complained about a piece of bologna.

"Someone has tampered with my fresh meat," she said, unimpressed.

"What makes you think that ma'am?"

"Look closely," she said and handed me the tube, "it's been cut in the middle."

I opened the tube of bologna and peered inside. Indeed, someone had carved the words "FUCK YOU" on the inside. *Wow*, I thought. *Whoever the artist is, they did a pretty good job with the carving.*

"Yes, ma'am, I do believe one of our staff tampered with your fresh meat product. I apologize on behalf of the store. Let's get you a refund and a new tube of bologna."

But she peered at me with her dark brown eyes.

"Actually, I want to know what you are going to do about this," she said.

I could understand her disappointment. She was a member of the First Nations community, as were many people who worked at the Superstore in Whitehorse. I had huge respect for the Indigenous peoples, who were often marginalized and dealing with all sorts of social issues. The store was a mess when I first got there, but it was something I could change. Just like Terrace, Whitehorse was a very tight-knit community. She would have known that I was new in town, and I wasn't gonna let her think I was trouble or didn't care about the people of Whitehorse. So, I asked for her number and said, "I will call you in a few days with an update."

When she left, I went to look at the daily schedule to see who had been working the previous shift. There had been two older ladies and a young man named Brian. There were no doubts about who the culprit was.

"It wasn't me," Brian shrugged once I had him in my office. I dangled the bologna in front of him like a floppy moose dick.

"So, you're telling me that Yolandi or Edith carved the words 'fuck you' into a piece of ham?"

"Yup."

"Well, fuck!" I exclaimed. "They did an incredible job."

His eyes narrowed.

"What are you talking about?"

"Every freaking letter was done perfectly! Incredible! You must have spent your whole shift doing this."

"Pfft..." he went, "I did that in five minutes, man."

"Of course you did," I chuckled. "Look, man, I'm not firing you, but you're under suspension for now. Let me talk to the union and a few other people and get back to you."

I wanted to do something for Brian, and I knew that the Yukon had loads of money to fund First Nations. So, I phoned the mayor and told him that I had this young man full of anger, but with an incredible talent. He called me back a few days later, and they said, "We want to come in and meet with you and Brian as well. I think we've got something."

So, the next day, I welcomed a small group of suited men to our office, where Brian was also waiting. The poor guy probably thought he was still in trouble. We all shook hands, and then we sat down.

"Well, Brian, it's certainly nice to meet you," the representative said. "We've been told you've got quite the talent when it comes to carving."

"Uh..." Brian's eyes shifted nervously around the room for a moment before he saw the smiles on our faces.

"What do you say about making it into a career?"

"Yeah... that would be great!" Brian said after taking it all in, "But you know... I can't go off to school or some course right now. I gotta work and make money!

"How much money are you making right now?" one of the suits asked.

"Sixteen dollars an hour."

"Ok, we can certainly match that while offering you a four-year scholarship for a carving course. We will also subsidize your food and rent."

Brian looked at me in bewilderment. Then a huge smile spread across his face, and he stood up and shook the director's hand. After they had left, I called the bologna lady with the good news. I have forgotten her name, but I hope she won't mind me calling her that. In any case, she seemed glad, and I felt good for giving back to the community.

A year on or so, I got a call from the director of the carving college again. He told me that Brian had been chosen as one of 18 people from all over Alaska and Yukon to attend a special First Nations-led course on an island in the Yukon River. He was to go there and learn how to carve out a canoe from a Cedar tree. In addition, they would also be offered alcohol and drug counseling, as well as mental health counseling from the Alaskan spirit men on the island. And, the director said, Brian wanted to invite me over to the island. I was stunned. Why me? He told me that they were going to hold a traditional ceremony where only one family member would be welcome to join, but Brian had no family who could come, so he had asked for me to come.

So, I boarded the boat that was going to take me across the river. I was the only white person on board, and I guessed that the other passengers were family members of the apprentices on the island. When we docked, we were greeted by a small welcoming committee, and I spotted Brian in the crowd. He looked great, sunburnt, tall, and proud - a far cry from the sulky teen that had worked for me a year prior. After welcoming us to the island, the apprentices and their family members started walking off.

"Where's everyone going?" I asked.

"On a tour around the island, to see what their kids are working on," Brian said.

"Are we going to?"

"Not yet."

So, we stayed on the beach. Two elders joined us with some instruments, one was playing the guitar, and the other one played violin. Both were chanting. It was beautiful, but it went on for a very long time. After about an hour and a half, I whispered to Brian, "What's going on?" And he whispered back, "You have to be family."

"I don't understand."

"You are being traditionally adopted."

I couldn't believe it. Being adopted into a community for which I had so much respect, made me feel so welcomed and at home; it brought tears to my eyes. My whole life, I had longed to belong somewhere, to be a part of a brethren. My need for camaraderie had taken me to places high and low, but the cultural adoption was the greatest honor. The whole community in Whitehorse knew about it. Later, once I had left the island, relatives of Brian told me they respected me so much that they would give me their late family members' status once they had passed on. It made me realize the impact my actions had and the importance of giving back to the community.

After completing his four-year apprenticeship, Brian had become a successful carver. He came by my office once, looking like a real man about town in his expensive clothes and million-dollar smile. He told me the Ontario government had provided him with a minimum of $50,000 worth of carvings a year. Now he had followed my lead and decided to give something back to society. To this day, Brian still makes me proud.

—

We had been foster parents for many years, and our first foster kids had now gone to live with their grandmother when we were approached once more. This time there was a family of four girls, and they were looking to rehome the oldest two. They had been in temporary housing, in many different homes. They had to move every two years not to get too attached to their host families. But now, the authorities were looking for something more permanent for them. We took them in when Kara was eight and Rachel was six. Taking kids in permanently was another huge step for our family. This time, we were in it for the long run. The girls got on brilliantly with the rest of the family, and although we occasionally faced challenges, they brought a lot of joy and love to our lives. But a few years later, we heard from the authorities again. The two younger sisters were homed with a different family, who had decided only to keep one, but to let the other one go. "She's too much trouble," they had said. The authorities explained to us, "If she doesn't get a new host family, she will go into a girls' house."

Once again, Tracy faced the challenge. Crystal had been described as a problem child, which could cause issues in an already huge family full of kids of different ages and abilities. But on the other hand, these "girl houses" were terrible places, riddled with violence and hostility. They were basically prisons for teenage girls. We couldn't have that on our conscience, so we decided to take her in.

The initial six months with Crystal were a shit show, to put it lightly. She was a real little manipulator who liked to stir the shit and got the other kids into trouble. When asked why, she just shrugged and said it was funny. When she wasn't mean to her siblings and foster siblings, she would try to annoy the adults around her. Tracy would never let me tell her off, knowing I was a pretty strong-worded guy. She was the soft, nurturing parent, whereas I was on the stricter side. But one day, I had had enough.

We had taken all the kids canoeing. I was in the same boat as Crystal and Peeky, with little Peeky sitting in the middle. Crystal was in the front of the canoe, and I was in the back, and she kept slamming her paddle and splashing Peeky until he cried. I kept saying, "Stop!" So, then she'd splash me instead while laughing gleefully.

"Okay," I said, "you need to stop."

"NOPE!" she cried loudly and splashed us some more.

"Right, Crystal, enough now!" I growled.

"Well, what are you gonna do about it?"

"I'm gonna rip that fucking life jacket off you. And I'm gonna toss you off the canoe."

She stopped and looked at me pensively and said: "You can't do that."

"Why not?"

"Because I don't know how to swim." She almost sounded scared. But then she hastily added: "And I'll drown, and you'll go to jail for murder."

"Well, that's where you're wrong, little girl. Have you seen your social services file? It's this fucking thick." I said and measured the air with my thumb and index finger. "I'll throw you off, and you'll drown. I'll go to the judge. I'll say that you drove me crazy. She will look at your file. She will say, 'Yeah, you're right.' She's gonna put me in a hospital and medicate me. And right now..." I said, "I'm fucking okay with that."

Crystal stopped splashing. She went completely quiet and didn't say anything else for the rest of that day.

Tracy was livid with me for scaring her, but I knew that sometimes when out of control, some kids need tough love. Bullying was not accepted in my household, and if someone acted a bully with no consequences, I would have to fight fire with fire. And it truly worked. I have never seen a person turn their life around so quickly. She never gave me lip again, and she stopped picking on her siblings. It was such a dramatic change in Crystal that the school got a hold of social services. They had to have a meeting with us.

"What did you guys do to turn this girl around?" they asked with big eyes.

I looked at Tracy, who just gave me the 'zip it' stare because she knew we couldn't tell them the truth.

"Oh, it's just the combination of having a loving and nurturing parent as well as a more... firm parent," Tracy assured them. They believed her. We couldn't tell them that she had met her match and that when pushed, I once again became that dragon that would burn any asshole to the ground if they stood in my way of happiness. I knew that Crystal was a great kid deep inside; she just needed a bit of tough love. To this day, Crystal is still living with us, and she is the most excellent, exuberant, adventurous young lady I've ever known. And one day, I know that all of my kids will do amazing things and give back to the world. I know that they will all make me as proud of them as I hope my parents were of me.

—

When I was 32 and Dakota was born, the doctors took him from us and ran out of the room. We soon found out he had been born with holes in his heart. He needed open heart surgery almost immediately, at only eight pounds, and he became the smallest baby in Canada to undergo such an operation. At the same time, my dad had heart problems and needed to undergo the same surgery. It was one of the most stressful and nerve-racking times in my life. Dakota came out of the surgery just fine, but my dad had five bypasses and then went into cardiac arrest. We nearly lost him.

Once he had healed, we had an emotional but candid conversation. Over the years, he had never approved of my lifestyle or clothes. I had always worn long sleeve t-shirts around him to cover up my body ink. But when he woke from his surgery, and I sat by his bed, he took my hand and said, "I don't give a rat's ass about what anyone thinks of you. The tattoos, the hair, the bikes. I don't care. I love you just the way you are, you are my son."

He was diagnosed with cancer twenty years later. He was 87 and chose not to fight it with chemotherapy. Instead, he wanted to go down the natural path and enjoy his final time with his family. The doctors gave him three to six months to live, and during that time our bond grew even stronger. It allowed us to have many conversations. At last I had the chance to tell him how grateful I was about the life he had given me and the amazing childhood he and Mom had provided for us. He passed away peacefully, surrounded by his family. My mother still lives in Parksville. I go to see her every week.

—

Twenty years after we tied the knot, Tracy and I were celebrating our anniversary with a trip to Las Vegas. The flight attendant came over with one flute of champagne and one flute of orange juice. I picked up the champagne and put it on Tracy's tray. She looked at me, smiled, picked it up, and put it back on my tray. And I just looked at her as if to say, what's that about? We were still raising kids, and Dakota was still only ten at the time.

But she just smiled at me and said: "Remember the deal we made? Well, you did it. So, drink up, and let's have some fun."

It was the first glass of champagne I had had in at least 18 years. After everything we had gone through, she knew she could trust me not to fall back into that black hole ever again. I didn't need to be kept on a leash; I was free to enjoy a glass of champagne on my 20th wedding anniversary. We clinked our glasses together.

"To the next twenty years!" we said, and laughed.

CHAPTER 10

*If Nothing Else,
Read This*

If my story has taught you anything, I hope it's about the importance of honest conversations. Not just about drugs, but life in general. I got the idea of writing this book when I was giving my youngest daughter, Jaz, a lift home from school. She was 13 at the time. She told me that a doctor had come to her school to talk to the pupils about drugs. "What did he say about it?" I asked. "He said that drugs were bad."

"Well, what else did he say?"

"Just that they were bad."

It made me realize that not much had changed since I was a kid. And I think I know why.

When we have children, our hearts leave our bodies, but no matter how closely we try to hold onto our kids, they will go off and form their own lives one day. We worry that we won't be able to protect them from all the dangers in the world, so we tell them horror stories about wolves in the woods and child-eating trolls. We tell them that drugs are bad, drinking is bad, and activities that might hurt them are also bad. We rarely offer nuanced or complete honesty to our children because we don't think that they can handle it.

Taking drugs feels amazing. That's why people do it, and that is why some people become addicted to drugs. It feels like going on a crazy rollercoaster, or even better, like being tied to a rocket going into space. The reason it feels so good is that the drugs, in this case, cocaine, affect the dopamine transporter in your brain so that dopamine accumulates in the synapse, which produces an amplified signal to the receiving neurons. This causes a feeling of euphoria. The feeling only lasts for about ten minutes, and when it starts to plummet, you begin to feel really low. Once you try it, you are likely to want to try it again. Like a rollercoaster.

Maybe the doctor who lectured about drugs to my daughter thought that if he likened cocaine to a rollercoaster, there would be a long line of 13-year-olds queueing up to do coke? Suppose he told them that taking drugs feels a lot like getting into the car of a rollercoaster. In that case, there would be the anticipation, where it all starts rumbling up and you're looking straight up into the sky, thinking, "Holy fuck. Holy fuck. Holy fuck. Holy fuck," and you finally get to the top in a dizzying moment — only to speed downhill back to earth with your ass up in your mouth, then spin around, thinking "Holy fuck, am I gonna die?". Would all kids immediately want to do cocaine?

When I was continuously using crack cocaine, I felt that I became more knowledgeable about the world. It was something I felt that I needed because, as a child, I had been lied to a lot for my protection. Cocaine will make you feel more enlightened, it will make you feel more energized and aware of your senses, all thanks to the chemical dopamine that is released in your brain. It was an incredibly interesting experience, but the real knowledge came from realizing that taking drugs does not necessarily make you a monster. I've got close friends, so close I consider them brothers, who do drugs and still enjoy their life. They are not bad people, nor scary or dangerous, they are beautiful human beings. They manage their life. They're knowledgeable about what they're doing, and I don't want them to stop. They are doing it responsibly, and I respect them for managing it. The truth is that all sorts of people use drugs, bankers, city mayors, teachers, writers, singers, grocery shop workers, parents, and even grandparents. A woman of 65 can become addicted to painkillers, and a boy of 17 can become addicted to meth.

But that does not mean that I want you to go out and get addicted to crack cocaine, Valium, alcohol, or any other drug. What I want is openness and honesty and an end to the stigma of drug addiction. A person who is addicted to narcotics is hurt in many ways, not just by the substance itself but by the stigma around the problem they are facing. We know it can happen to anyone, young or old, poor or rich, black or white. Addiction is not something that is just happening to people who are weak or vulnerable; neither is someone's fate written in the stars. It happened to me, despite my safe and happy childhood, despite my loving relationship with my wife, and despite being a proud dad. And if people were more open about it, you might find out that it has happened to people you look up to, a friend or an idol. Ending the stigma starts with complete honesty, and I hope we can be franker in our conversations about drugs in the future. There are those who can manage taking drugs recreationally from time to time, and there are those who are ruining their lives with addiction. Those who need to quit should feel safe to seek treatment without the fear of judgment from society or their loved ones.

When I was at my lowest, I stared into my three-year-old son's eyes, and I knew that my way of living was selfish and that I needed to quit. I was lucky to have a sister who had been there too, who didn't call me names or think of me as a monster. She took me in and let me heal, and that was what I needed. I was also lucky to have a wife who never gave up on me. If she had decided that I could never see my kids again, it is possible that I would have been stuck in the addiction because I would not have had a reason to quit.

But the truth is that we cannot and should not have to rely on family to help us through or out of addiction. Not everyone has parents, a partner or even friends to rely on. In my opinion, the healthcare system needs to be improved. One of my friends had a son, the same age as Peeky, who struggled with heroin abuse. I tried to help him several times. His mother sent him to detox, but when he came out, there was no support system in place for him. So, he fell back into using again. The same thing happened the second time he went to detox, and the third time he was rejected at the door, just like me. It was a Friday evening, and after being told "no" he just disappeared into the night. His mother got a lawyer who told them that they couldn't refuse to help him. So the detox center let them know that a bed would be ready for him two days later, on a Sunday morning. When his mother finally found him, he was in the middle of using drugs. He became unconscious, and they ended up taking him to jail, as it was deemed the only safe place for him, the only alternative to the detox center while waiting for an available bed. They ensured his mother that they had trained people to watch over him. They left him in the jail cell for 11 hours without checking on him. When they found him, his heart rate had gone so low that he was in a coma. By the time they tried to bring him out of the coma, he was gone. Nothing had changed in 30 years since I was in that situation. Addicts are still left to die. That is the ugly truth.

I don't believe in lying to children. They may not understand everything, but they understand more than we think. What really makes children stand out is that they don't judge. Their hearts are open and untainted by bias and judgment, unlike adults. Only recently, I cut my thumb while working. I cut it open so badly that I could see bone. It was two o'clock in the morning because I was working night shift. Tracy took me to the emergency in Montreal, and I was in there for two hours before anyone would even talk to me. When a nurse finally looked at my finger, he asked me how it happened. When I explained that I cut it while cutting stock at work, he exclaimed, "Oh you work? We thought you had been in a street fight. That's why we let you wait."

They had taken one look at my long beard and tattoos and decided that I wasn't worthy of healthcare. But children aren't ruined by prejudice, and that is why we can talk to them.

I talk to my children about drugs, they know what I have been through, and I have complete honesty with them. I don't believe in trying to control what my children do, but I do believe in arming them with knowledge and trust. Drugs are everywhere in our society today, and many young people are going to try drugs regardless of whether their parents have tried to scare them off or not. I would rather my children knew what they were and how they affect you than just be told they're "bad" with no context. I don't want us to use scaremongering to stop our kids from trying drugs, I want to give them the knowledge to make better decisions and to have a better life. At some point, my kids' friends will be trying drugs and they might be tempted. I want to be able to share my knowledge about everything that I have experienced so that they can go into those situations more knowledgeable, more confident, and safer. I would never want my children, or any children, to go through what I went through, so my deal with my kids is: "Anything you want to try, do it with me, and we'll do it in a safe form. And if you don't wanna do it with me, you really should think twice about why you want to do it in the first place."

My youngest son, Peek, put it to me in a very clever way. He said, "It's like when you hang out with your friends, and they're train surfing. You're at the station, and the train is about to take off. It's moving really slowly at first, and that's when they jump onto it. But your parents have told you your whole life not to play with trains because it will kill them, so you hesitate. And you see your friends smiling and laughing, having the time of their life, and you're scared you'll be excluded from the experience and the whole friendship with those kids. So now the train is speeding up, and you're jumping. But because you hesitated out of insecurity, the train is now moving too fast, and you slip and end up underneath it.

I would hate to see someone I love fall victim to drug abuse, but I watched people jump on that train with no issues and no repercussions, and it rocked my world as I had been told my whole life that it would kill you. I didn't see the risks and the possibilties until I jumped on that train myself.

If you love someone with addiction issues, there are many things you can do to support them. Addiction, like cancer, often comes in four stages. It begins with experimenting, goes on to regular use, to high-risk use, to total dependency. The best thing you can do is to read up on the type of drug they are using, and the addiction process that comes with it. Arm yourself with knowledge and try to have an honest and open conversation with them about it. Being close to someone with addiction issues is likely to make your life harder, especially if it is your spouse or parent, so make sure to seek help for yourself. Remember that you often can't force or coerce someone into seeking specialist treatment, and although they may be a person close to you, unless they are your child, it is not your responsibility to save them. It is also not your responsibility to lie for them or protect them when their substance abuse problem gets them into trouble. This will likely just enable them.

Instead, let them know that you will be there for them every step of the way when they are ready to seek treatment. And remember that the most important thing of all is to show compassion. Drug addicts already face enough stigma from society, but if they know you are there for them and believe that they can get better, at least they will have a reason to get clean. Stigma is one of the barriers that can prevent addicts from seeking professional help, so your best bet is to help end it. Instead, let them know that they are loved. Love and support offer hope, and you can't win any battles without hope.

If you are someone struggling with addiction issues, please know that I have been there too, and I don't judge you. I didn't write this book with the intention of telling you what to do. I just want to share my story and hopefully inspire you to take action. If you want to find a way out of the darkness, you need to break free from the prison that is currently keeping you in addiction. Had I not isolated myself from the community where drugs were normalized and given out freely, I don't know if I would have been able to stop. For me, it was a hotel and a town. For you, it might be a relationship, a friendship group, or a family. Your first step is to remove yourself from any bad influence and any person or entity if they are enabling your addiction. Some might wish to go to rehab, but not everyone will have that opportunity, so in that case, going to stay with a relative or sober friend in a different part of the country is also an option. Go away somewhere where you can be safe, and your journey to recovery can start there. You will be at war with your brain, and it will be hard. You will be a small fish, swimming upwards in a heavy downward stream. Don't have any expectations of yourself at this point; remember that just getting through the day without drugs or alcohol is enough. Once you're a little bit more functional, try to find something to keep you busy. For me, it was a job. And then, it's time to make a deal with your brain. When I was at my lowest, I knew I couldn't quit cold turkey. So, I thought to myself: *I am not quitting. I am simply pausing until I have raised my kids. They take priority right now,* *and once they're all grown up, I can go back to using again.* The problem with quitting cold turkey is that you're making an unrealistic promise to yourself and the people around you. You are not vowing to take the first steps of your journey; you are vowing to climb Kilimanjaro. When you are addicted to drugs, the drugs are all that matter. Therefore, the notion that you will never touch them again can feel like a threat to your body. You need to know that once you have accomplished a task, such as waiting for a few years, you can be rewarded again.

So, I told my brain a lie, and thirty years later, I still have to lie to my brain. I am 55 years old, my children have reached legal age, and now I have grandkids, so I still can't go back to using. I will have to wait another fifteen years. And maybe I'll keep tricking my brain because that is what works for me. I made the choice to try crack cocaine in my twenties, and over thirty years later, I am still feeling the effects of it. And although I have been clean for decades with a successful career and a lovely family, I am still, occasionally, swimming upstream. And if you are, too, I hope you can find comfort in knowing that you are not swimming alone.

I'm not anti-drug, I'm not pro-drug. I'm pro-sharing my experience and knowledge and putting the moose on the table. It starts with honesty and the courage to talk about difficult topics. It starts with trust in the new generation because if we can't trust our children, how will they ever learn to trust us?

Tracy's Words

When Freddie first started using crack cocaine, it was such a shock to me. We were new parents, best friends, and so much in love. Then it all happened so quickly. Luckily, I had a great support network around me, so I was able to separate myself from him. He was going through whatever he was going through, and at the time, I thought of him as being on this "vacation."

Of course, there were times when I hated him. I just felt so betrayed and had to turn him off. I was raising our kids while working hard as a barmaid in the pub down the road from him, so I would hear things through the grapevine. But I was never going to be the person to keep him away from his kids because he was and still is a great father.

I clearly recall a conversation I had with my dad at the time, "You must really love him." I don't think he meant it in a judgmental way, it was just an observation. But he was right. Although I felt betrayed, I chose never to give up on him. I loved him too much, and my love was too pure. Whenever he needed me, I took him to detox. I dropped everything and ran to him when he needed me. I baked for him and took care of him when he'd let me. I just wanted him to be well, and it was hard to watch him disintegrate.

Once he made that call to Ramona and managed to leave Nanaimo, I closed the door on the past. I wanted to move forward and rebuild our life together and forget all that had happened. Any mention of his time as an addict triggered me. So we never really spoke about it, and I never really knew the details of it, until I read this book. It has been amazing and pretty wonderful to read it all and be part of it. And now I realize how it was for him. All this time, I thought he was just being selfish, because I didn't fully fathom what the drugs were doing to his brain. It also made me see how I have judged drug abusers in the past, although I am sad to say it. I think Freddie has had a huge breakthrough that I didn't even understand needed to happen.

Through the years, we have watched friends go through similar turmoil with drug addiction. It's such heartbreak watching the demise of a young person, and you think you can somehow fix it, but you can't. All you can do is listen and open the conversation.

Insights

1. Don't fall for peer pressure. You don't need to impress anybody but yourself.

2. The truth has a way of coming out. Lies have consequences and can ruin lives.

3. Have the conversation, even if it makes you uncomfortable.

4. You don't need to tick every box in the job description to apply. Just show up and demonstrate how willing you are to learn and how eager you are to go the extra mile.

5. Life is too short not to work for something. A better future, a better salary, a better position. Even if your job is tedious or feels meaningless, make sure to work hard, and you will be rewarded.

6. The guy sitting next to you on the bus with long hair and tattoos could be a drug addict. But he can also be the CEO of a successful company. Or someone who regularly carries out volunteer work. *"Judge not, that ye be not judged."*

7. Treat people with respect and make sure they respect you back. Don't accept abuse and ill-treatment just because you are in an inferior position.

8. Everybody wants to belong somewhere and to be respected and loved. The place where this matters the most is within your own family and closest circle. The need to impress the "cool kids" will bite you in the ass.

9. The best way to earn the respect and love of others is by helping them.

10. Sometimes, some people need a bit of tough love.

11. A life-changing moment can alter how you see the world and help you accept the small things that bother you.

12. Addicts are ill. Addiction is an illness. Most addicts don't want to be in that situation but have landed there because of various factors. Consider this before treating them as lesser than someone with any other illness.

13. Just smiling at a homeless person on the street can help take away the stigma of drug addiction.

14. If someone you love is battling drug addiction, listen to them and try to understand them, but don't enable their behavior, and if they get into trouble, let them take accountability.

15. If someone close to you is addicted to drugs, remember to seek help for yourself too.

On Quitting Drugs

1. Isolate yourself from anyone who can provide you with drugs.

2. Don't give up on getting help, even if you feel let down by the system. You are entitled to help.

3. Cocaine affects the dopamine transporter in your brain so that dopamine accumulates in the synapse, which produces an amplified signal to the receiving neurons. This causes a feeling of euphoria. This is why it feels so good to do drugs. The feeling only lasts for about ten minutes, and when it starts to plummet, you begin to feel low. In other words, your brain tricks you into thinking good things are happening, which is why cocaine is so addictive.

4. Take one day at a time. Don't make unrealistic promises to yourself.

5. Give yourself time to heal, even if all you do is eat and sleep for weeks.

6. Talk to people who have been there. Talk to your friends and family members you trust.

7. Don't be afraid to show people who you really are. Honest and open conversations bring us closer together.

8. Quitting drugs can feel like falling to earth and having to walk the streets with demons after flying high with the gods. Reality hits hard, but it is worth it.

9. To motivate yourself, tell yourself you're only quitting for *x* amount of time. Once you've reached your goal, set a new timeline. Keep telling yourself you can go back, but not just yet.

10. Don't fear judgment. Some people won't like you, but you will survive.

11. Find something that will keep you occupied and brings you meaning.

12. Sharing is powerful. Think of all the people you can inspire and help with your story.

13. Accept that you might have to live with your addiction for the rest of your life, but you can still be in control of your actions and the quality of your life.

14. You are not alone. I have been there too.

15. Scaremongering won't keep young people off drugs. Honesty is key.

16. If you find someone down, offer a helping hand. If they accept it, pull hard to help them, but if they start to pull you down with them, let go.

Acknowledgements

To my dad, I thank you for your advice and motivation before you left. You urged me to tell others my story, and your words "Just be you, Freddie "and "The only thing you can do wrong is not being yourself" whispered in my ears throughout this entire process. I told you I didn't think I would have the means to write a book, yet the opportunity to do so dropped on my plate less than a year after you left. A coincidence? I don't think so. I hope I do you proud.

I would like to thank my best friend and wife, Tracy, for your decades of support and love, my kids for bringing a bigger meaning to my life, my mom for continuing to be a pillar in my life, and my 2009 HD Road King for keeping me young and sane.

Special thanks to Aaron and Sofia and the team at We Write Stories; working with you was like going on a long road trip on the bike.

To Sarah Hook-Nilsson for your editing, feedback, and suggestions, thank you!

To Laura, for your amazing artwork, thank you!

Lastly, a big thanks to Peeky for our long, detailed conversations throughout this entire process. You're an amazing person. Thank you!

Exhibit A

The Epilogue

Dear reader,

I want to provide a disclaimer that the information in Chapter 2, is based on my recollection of events that occurred when I was a child or is based on information that I have been told. There is no way to prove the validity of all statements told to me.

I was made aware after the initial release of my book that many of the events in Chapter 2 were not wholly accurate. Government records do not indicate that my sisters assaulted anyone or that they were arrested.

Lastly, I want to note that I never personally witnessed my sisters' using drugs but was instead told that they did through rumors in my community and my parents' speculation. The twins did not use drugs and were never addicts. This book was not made with the intention of hurting anyone in my family.

About the Author

Freddie is a free-spirited, big-hearted, father of three and father to five. He is a loving husband and the lifelong friend of his wife, Tracy. He is a reformed drug addict, ready to offer a helping hand to anyone who is struggling to find their way out of addiction. His tremendous respect for others, his non-judgemental attitude, and his own hard work ethic, are an inspiration for all who are keen to enhance the lives of others.

He currently works as a manager for a contracting company of retail specialists in British Columbia and travels Canada to promote and encourage others.

He still makes time for bike rides on his Harley Davidson with childhood friends and family, as well as camping, hiking, and travelling.

Freddie grew up in Terrace, BC, and currently resides in Courtney on Vancouver Island, British Columbia.

www.ingramcontent.com/pod-product-compliance
Lightning Source LLC
Chambersburg PA
CBHW051627120626
46551CB00014B/1964